# IZARI

## Keith Casburn

Published by
Light Publishing

First published in 1996
by Light Publishing
The College of Psychic Studies
16 Queensberry Place
London, SW7 2EB

Made in the United Kingdom

ISBN 0 903336 12 X (paperback)

The aim of LIGHT PUBLISHING and THE COLLEGE OF
PSYCHIC STUDIES is to explore all aspects of spiritual and
psychic knowledge.

The views expressed in all books published by LIGHT
PUBLISHING and THE COLLEGE OF PSYCHIC STUDIES
are those of the author, and do not necessarily reflect the
views of The College of Psychic Studies.

"We have room for all who realise the importance, in a
materialistic age, of expressing a belief that there is
something behind matter and that death does not end all. . ."
*From a preliminary meeting of the College, November 1883. This
was the declared note of the then new College and it remains so to
this day.*

Typeset, printed and bound in Great Britain
by Whitstable Litho, Whitstable, Kent.

# CONTENTS

# BIOGRAPHY

Keith Casburn was born and raised in Galway, Republic of Ireland. He spent two years studying general science at University College, Galway before training as an actor in the UK. He spent eleven years working in theatre and television as an actor and director before being drawn into Executive Search as a research consultant. Two years prolonged illness finally brought him into an understanding of himself, his psychic gifts and healing potential. He has been working full time as a psychic and healer since 1991.

# ACKNOWLEDGEMENTS

Christine McCarroll –who once again transcribed all the tapes.

Charles Duff – my editor who managed to plough his way through the maze and made sense of the seeming incomprehensible.

Polly Rathbone – for her visual concept of what the book represents.

Ruth Mayo – for the proofreading and advice.

Oliver Rathbone – for creating the mechanism that puts this out into the world.

Dudley Poplak – for giving a mouthpiece to my work.

Jenny Grant – for having enough faith in me and this text to allow it to be published.

# ASK

# FOREWORD

It's that time of morning when I give myself an opportunity to quiet the mind and try to find that place within me that is neutral, where nothing happens. For some reason, it has always been easy for me to empty the mind of everything and to be able to walk around with 'an empty head'. I always used to equate this with not being intelligent, but then I used to confuse intelligence with knowledge and it is only the last few years that I view the capacity to achieve this state as being valuable. How can we possibly understand what is possible, if we continually allow ourselves to be limited by what we believe? To journey beyond knowledge itself, surely, is the greatest adventure.

But back to that morning. A lightening around my head, a sense of upliftment and spheres of brilliant gold begin to accumulate above me, gradually being drawn down towards my shoulders, leaving the apex of my body immersed in a pulsating light. For several minutes it seems the structure of my skull is becoming diffuse, so this pulsating light has free access to the mass of my brain. Now there is no time or space, merely a fusion of a variety of vibratory impulses creating equally a sense of excitement, doubt, clarity and anticipation of something about to happen. The usual insecurities immediately flash through my mind – is this real, am I really losing my sanity this time, can I trust what is happening, will it be coherent and of value? Doubts, the reflections of my subjective reality, are quickly eroded as the pulsating starts to bring with it words. Not sentences, just words. Strangely, as there is a pulsation by my left ear there is also a word placed in my head from that direction. Another pulsation above my head causes a further word to enter from that place – and so it continues. Word follows word. Never have I experienced anything like this. It is difficult to describe but the sentences (what else can I call them?) don't begin or end, they are just there. I feel them before I hear them, but the words, when they arrive, are still surprising.

In retrospect, I don't recall much of what was said except – 'We are Izaris.' 'Communication will come through Sauris'. Neither of these meant anything at the time. Izaris sounded similar to Lazaris, the consciousness channelled through Jach Pursel, which I had enjoyed reading several years previously. Was it that which was coming up from the deep recesses of my mind that I had misheard, or something else? Although I trust my ability to communicate, I still have reservations about the substance and origins of some of the information until it proves either conclusive or understandable. However, I was left with the feeling of being opened up to a very different level of consciousness that had not previously been available. A physical rather than a spiritual consciousness.

The dome of light intensity remained around my head and shoulders for some time, but the pulsing stopped. No further information, which was perplexing. Why? Always, why?

Brenda Marshall, the then President of the College of Psychic Studies, gave me a book to review for LIGHT magazine. It was called 'Starlight Elixirs and Cosmic Vibrational Healing'. It was about how the light energy from certain stars had been captured in liquid solutions and used in a similar way to homeopathic preparations. I took the book home, put it on the bookcase and promptly forgot about it for a couple of months until Brenda reminded me about the review. With great embarrassment I promised to do it very quickly for her. I arbitrarily opened the book and my heart suddenly started to pound as I went into shock. Staring me in the face was a mini chapter about the star Izar, Epsilon Bootis, one of the second dimension stars in the heavens, and what properties it had to offer us mere mortals. Roughly, it commented on how some people who had difficulty in transforming their own inspirational energy into physical energy frequently suffered from Chronic Fatigue Syndrome. The use of the energy from this star could be helpful in shifting this. The synchronicity started falling into place. Without going into too much detail, I myself had suffered from ME for about eighteen months. Today many people come to me suffering from the same debilitating condition. A combination of colour healing and acupuncture opened all my psychic faculties, which made me conscious of my mediumistic and healing abilities and allowed me to overcome my illness completely. Now all the proof I had been waiting for was suddenly available.

The real rapport with Izaris began in earnest now. Regular dialogues occurred to explain and clarify its purpose and its need to express itself openly to the world so that others could experience what is represented. Those readers who have heard me speak in public will be familiar with my saying how paralysing I find it. Now I was being asked again to let this flow through me in public. So I took the opportunity to let this happen selectively in certain workshops, but it seemed more was required. I needed to create a similar situation that brought about 'Principles of the Universe', my previous book, namely, a series of dialogues within the College of Psychic Studies, in a ten week time scale. I was given the date when this should commence and that it would also be put into book form and would be published. Doubting Thomas refused to believe or accept this. The idea appalled me and I put it to one side and refused to do it. At least, that is what I thought I was doing.

Throughout the year I began to feel increasingly edgy and restricted. A pressure was building around me that seemed to limit everything I was doing. Surprise, surprise, a staff member at the College mentioned that several people had been asking whether I would do a similar course to the one that brought 'Principles of the Universe' to life. Reluctantly, I sat down and wrote a programme called 'Cosmology in Motion' and gave it to the College for approval which it received. Strangely, I immediately felt better both physically and mentally, and suddenly that edginess was gone. The context of my work altered, acquired a better fluidity, and I began to relate to it more easily. Izaris burst onto the scene again with more information as to how I was to prepare for the beginning of the course.

This now brings you, the reader, to the book itself. It came out of the weekly sessions that were attended by twenty stalwarts at the College of Psychic Studies. These people managed to magnetise this information from me. For some reason, it needed a group energy to be able to hold this, otherwise it wouldn't really have been possible. The process was demanding for them and for me. We were all very glad when the course had ended as we felt we couldn't take any more. The concentration was enormous, the information was quite dense and often difficult to relate to and it was physically demanding in a way that isn't easily explained; like having an enormous meal, then needing to go to bed to sleep it off. Sleeping had never been more pleasurable.

Since that time, apart from incidental workshops, I haven't done any courses or led any classes. It was so cathartic, I required complete and utter rest. The freedom this brought has allowed me to do other things and to put my foot in the water of the real world again. To date I have had two years away from teaching. However, as I write this, I am beginning to be drawn back into teaching, but in a more pragmatic way. Retrospectively, Izaris drew me into the stars and allowed me to see what is really there. For that I am eternally grateful.

This book isn't important, as it is my experience alone, and those who trusted me enough to bring them to experience it for themselves. If you, the reader, can gain some of that magic for yourself, then this book will have some validity at least.

People ask me if I channel. The answer is no. I developed as a medium. I am clairvoyant and clairaudient. My contact with Izaris is clairaudient. I hear the information then speak it, reaching a point where I no longer hear, as the flow of information passes through me in an uninterrupted way. It does not pass through my conceptual mind. I hear the information but don't listen to it, otherwise I would start evaluating what is being said and may wish to alter it. The challenge for any medium or psychic is to say what is there. The need to relate to that would be to put it in the context of your own experience, which would be wrong. Hence the need for trust. The discipline for any developing psychic is to raise the vibration or potential of the conceptual mind to such a level that anything can enter into it. That is all. If nothing enters, there is nothing to communicate. Should a flow develop, knowing that it does relate to something or someone specific requires understanding and patience, as it isn't always possible to relate to it at that moment. Trusting that the psychic mechanism does work and is valid is imperative. The demands made by those who consult a medium leave no room for doubt. Rightly or wrongly, you can only give what is there.

I have no illusions about the vagueness that can surround any form of spiritual or cosmic communication. As the book 'Izaris' is now being made available to a public audience, know that it is not presented as a definitive guide or précis of what is about to happen. It is imperative that the reader remains intelligent and open minded. If the material provokes thought and extends perception, it will have served its purpose. It is important that, as we enter into a seeming phase of accelerated learning, we don't get caught up in the trap of becoming too comfortable with our surroundings and our beliefs. Society and contemporary structures are changing too rapidly for us to feel too secure for too long. To have security within what we sense and feel is all that we really need. So let us try and develop that in order to know that we can deal with whatever comes our way. We are basically capable, are we not?

# ONE

## *The Being*

To feel encouragement, to feel warmth, that state has to be created in the vessel to allow the passage through him to be received with warmth and compassion. Your vessel, in this case, in speaking to you before he allows what is present to come through, is merely laying low any expectation that he may have of himself in relation to what will be said over the coming weeks. For him to be able to lay aside anxiety and allow himself to achieve a sense of detachment is important not only for him but for us. We have wanted to speak for some time. There has been lack of synchronicity for this to take place up until today. This is due to no fault, merely to do with circumstance and the emotional development that has effected your vessel.

We greet you then with warmth, and understanding. We speak from a point within the universe that is physically at a great distance. In our continued relationship with your vessel, in a way that he is not consciously aware of, there has been a very specific development as he has been continually brought to different vibrational points to allow him to hold within his psyche and within his physical body vibrations that actually displace emotion and feeling. This, in a very crude way, brings about not only a sense of emotional displacement, but some degree of stress. Not that you need to be unduly concerned for him, but merely understand that to arrive at this point of communication there is a process through which he has gone to allow him to come to the point when he can actually sit back, relax and allow this communication to take place in the first instance.

There has been communication from us before, in a specific circumstance, in this building. We are about to identify ourselves in terms of name and in terms of consciousness. It is important that you do not identify this name with a personality, as we are sure a lot of you already understand that sounds have mathematical connotations which, in vibrational terms, have specific resonances in terms of time and in terms of place within the physical universe. So to identify us as a specific source, while this is accurate in the context of how we are relating now, has, outside of this context, no real meaning or value.Once this particular discourse has finished, our relationship with you, and our relationship with your vessel is terminated and the complex coming together of sound, of colour, of intensity, shifts into a very specific non-specificity; so that, in your terms, it no longer exists, it breaks up, it blends with other vibratory forces, it becomes part of other consciousness forms.

We give ourself the name Izaris, this in your alphabet, I - Z - A - R - I - S. What your vessel was explaining in terms of having contact with us initially relates to the star Izar which is present in your visible galaxy. Izaris means stemming from the star; that the form of consciousness represented stems

2

from the star Izar. You need not confuse this with there being life-form, as you understand it, on the star Izar, merely that this is a point in vibratory space that has a particular magnetic attraction to it; that draws to it a certain vibratory context, consciousness, if you like, that has specific meaning and value. This, for all practical terms, has a very specific relationship to your constitution, to how your body works in terms of the fluid state within the body which has particular relevance to the element potassium and which bears specific relationship to the balance or electronic charge that you have within the cell itself, so that we, Izaris, relate very directly to the constitutional state within the cell itself. So, as we speak to you, we have to establish a relationship within the cellular memory of your vessel, which is then going to appeal to the cellular memory that you have contained within each of you.

Understand, therefore, that because you are all at different stages of evolutionary development and, as you have within you different origins of your own wisdom, so the way that we relate to each of you in turn is going to be markedly different. What you understand from what we say is going to be different. How you interpret and relate to what is said in your own personal circumstances is going to be unique in terms of you and your relationship with yourself. You may try to compare your reaction to that of others present in the room, and you may find that there will be certain circumstances where there is an overlap or a sense of commonality in the way you relate to what is said, but, conversely you will find that your perceptions of what is evoked in you will also be very, very different. Each is valid, each is real, and each is truthful in its own way. As your vessel is very keen to say again and again, in what he describes as the evolving metaphor, what you hear is right for you at that point in time. You don't have to accept it, you don't have to deny it.

Understand it at the level that it is given. Don't feel that you have to do anything with what is said today or over the coming weeks, merely observe it, experience it at the level that it is given and then feel free to forget everything that has been said. Merely allow yourself to vibrate in the words, to experience what it will evoke in you, for over the coming weeks we will endeavour to describe feelings, attitudes, emotional relationships that you feel dominate your life, giving you a greater sense of freedom perhaps, allowing you to feel less guilty about what your feelings are saying to you, allowing you to look outside your conditioned behaviour more. If we remove or enable you to step outside of any guilt, of any obligation, then something has been achieved that is very important. As a race you are habitual. As a race you are exacting on yourselves and often very judgemental of what you do, and it is this judgemental quality that often inhibits action, so you, as a result, get caught up in re-action, merely reacting to what you have around you, to what is said, to what is communicated, to what society and people demand of you rather than what you yourself feel you need to demand of yourself. This is very important.

Within society as it is structured now, what all are experiencing is a certain loosening within that structure. Now if we look at structure in terms of what you think and what you believe, it creates very specific beliefs which, in turn, set out concrete parameters, within which you feel you have to operate in a very deliberate way. If we go to an extreme so that you envisage a scenario where there are absolutely no parameters whatsoever, the sense of being abandoned, the sense of where do I look then if there are no parameters, becomes too much. So that somewhere in terms of your evolutionary development as spiritual beings it is required to find a focus where there is some suggestion at least of where these parameters might be, to give you some sort of direction and clarity. So at least there is a motivation towards something, even if, when you reach the end of the journey, that something doesn't exist. Because what you then have, if the journey has been experienced in an unconditional and unrestrictive way, may actually give rise to something that is even more progressive, more illuminating and less restrictive than what you have already experienced.

To come back is, for us, a risk. We are part of the stars. We, in crude terms, are a platform in free space which acts as a receiver of information. We, in terms of Izaris, are not the communicator. This is facilitated by, in your language, a translator. We can give you the name of this translator. Again, please remember that there is no defined personality and the name that we are going to give merely reflects the vibratory state of this being. In time, as science can allow itself to understand the consciousness that is contained within vibratory states of being, it will come to understand more the nature of the words that are given. The translator has the name Sauris represented by the letters S - A - U - R - I - S. So, your communicator is Sauris, but the communicator receives this information from Izar. We, as we identify ourselves as Izaris, are the hardware. Sauris is the software. This is where you can establish an emotional relationship with the information that is given. Without Sauris, what is said would be very cold. Izar, the consciousness Izaris, has no emotion as you understand it. It is totally detached. It has no real experience or understanding of your emotional state of being. Sauris, if we look at the letters that compose the composite nature of this name, means that although this translator comes from a point energetically beyond Izar, the accumulation of the vibratory forces: light, sound, and intensity, has greater understanding of emotional states than have we. We are speaking as though we are Izaris rather than Sauris, and that is how it will be. When it is difficult for us to communicate, there will be a transfer in terms of energy from Izar to Sauris, so that the communication will be less interrupted, less static, so there will be a greater flow, as Sauris can empathise more with your language, with what needs to be communicated.

We wish to explain our relationship with your vessel, and we are doing this to enable you to understand the universality of what this relationship means, so that you can identify, if you like, for yourselves, the repercussions that this has for you. We wish to explain the change in the constitution of your vessel. As we are sure you are already aware, the vibratory body you have around you creates the physical body. Any change in the state of that energy body requires the physical body to respond. If the physical doesn't respond, there is a breakdown in the relationship between the physical and the energy blueprint.

When we look at cellular memory, what we have, simply, is emotion. That is all that there is, three states of being: the emotional, which you equate as the physical; the spiritual, the non-physical counterpart of your emotional state, which represents the reality or the transformational state that you enter into when the physical body dies and, when there is no further need for the spiritual state, you reach the third state, when the consciousness that is essentially you makes a quantum leap into a new level of being that is contained within the cosmic. We originate from the cosmic. Look on the cosmic as the blueprint of all. When we relate, therefore, to Sauris, we relate to an energy device that in itself relates to your spiritual, which, remember, is the non-physical counterpart of your emotional being. So, as far as we are concerned, the spiritual is just another part of your emotional experience. The ability that enables Sauris to relate to this emotional being then, is great. But do understand that this spiritual emotional being has no physical context, that there is less density than your physical state. So the ability for that spiritual state to have relationships with other consciousness-forms is markedly better than you in your dense physical state.

As the energy body, your aura, evolves and grows into something finer, what you as humans experience is an uncomfortableness in your emotional state of being. You try to reason: Why do I feel uncomfortable? You try to justify what you are feeling in relation to people and to circumstance. How often, we ask, do you formulate the question in your mind: Is what I feel related only to my state of being? Is what I feel to do with a sense of involvement? Or to be more specific: I know my aura responds to something else far beyond my perception but, within the physical reality, I am having difficulty trying to come to terms with my dense, physical, emotional state and its relationship with my spiritual, auric state. Remember, this whole domain still relates to feeling and emotion. Within spiritual reality, as you define it, there is still feeling, there is still emotion. There is still an understanding that, as you move through time, as you move from life to life, as you move from life to non-life, there is a sense of progression, a sense of continuity of experience and understanding, and this is for a very good reason. This experience and understanding will always be, not exclusively but largely, within the emotional state. So you, reincarnating on earth to experience further feelings in the human condition, further emotions in your human compassionate state, have a sense of continuity, and it is important that this is recognised and acknowledged. That does not exclude your being able to step outside the psychospiritual into the cosmic, both in your conscious state and in your spiritual state as well. What we have is the possibility of consciousness being able to leave the emotional altogether and to go into a totally non-emotional, neutral state of being. To gain progressive understanding and to bring that progressive understanding, namely the spiritual, back to the emotional state, so that, within the spiritual context, there can be preparation, to enable consciousness-form to enter a physical body once more without there being some breakdown in communication. In your terminology, the reticence of the spirit to enter the physical because of what it knows it needs to communicate or to experience, becomes so strong that it makes the experience of that particular life almost redundant.

What your vessel experiences is difficulty in maintaining an emotional relationship with himself. Consequently within him there is often sadness for which there is no rational or logical explanation. This sadness is merely do to with the sense of displacement of the emotional body that surrounds him as it experiences a total sense of isolation. This, in vibratory terms, is to allow part of the cosmic vibration to blend with his emotional being in such a way that doesn't deny him feeling. He will freely talk about this so we feel we are not laying bare a secret that needs to be kept secret. He has been offered an opportunity to step outside his emotional being altogether while still maintaining a physical presence on the earth. This he has very firmly rejected as he has felt that his commitment to certain people and to certain situations means that what can be said can be recognised with a greater sense of truth and emotional empathy. Although empathising is not something that your vessel does nor is it something that he needs to experience. Within his cellular memory, therefore, the protein-restructuring that is taking place within his DNA – as the helix and the bonds that establish firm context within the DNA become connected with greater emphasis – means that it is difficult for him to be able to maintain cellular structure. What we have, therefore, is a breakdown within the densest part of his physical structure, namely the skeleton or the bones. This also, as we move into less dense structure, namely the connective tissue within the body, means that often there is absence of sensibility. When we come into the softer tissue in the body, it frequently means that the absorptive properties within the soft tissue also start to break down. The important factor within the constitution is the need to stimulate and propagate the electronic charge within the cell, looking at the process of osmosis within the body, namely the way that material passes through the body from an aqueous solution that is dense to an aqueous solution that is less dense. If there is any imbalance in the charge within that cellular structure, it often means that there is a sense of retention within the cells, as the fluid cannot continue its journey through the very specific region that it needs to pass through. What helps maintain this is consistent contact with a vibratory consciousness that is beyond physical vibration; being increasingly aware of the balance of calcium and potassium within the body; being very alert to diet as the diet can often change on a daily basis. By diet we mean, what is comfortable to pass through. What today may be nourishing, tomorrow may be poison, the following day may be more acceptable, and the day after that may have no further use within your diet.

So the sense of turmoil he feels, as he relates to what we are as Izaris, is difficult. Even when he is not relating directly to what we represent, he has established within himself something progressive that can no longer retrace its steps.

He's in free space, he has been given a push and to go back would, in cellular-structural terms, bring about a total collapsing of the cell. It would, therefore, bring about a total destruction of the body. As we are describing certain cellular characteristics and constitutional processes that are beginning to alter within his body, we say to you, recognise these changes within yourself. We take a moment to acknowledge each person in this room, and we recognise the changes that each of you is experiencing within cellular and constitutional progress. The need for you to be alert to your own constitutional and dietary needs in relation to what we have said, therefore, is quite important. Mainly to be alert to what feels comfortable when you eat and when you drink. That is all. And not to restrict yourself and think, today I can't eat a specific food. Allow yourself from time to time to go back to that food if the desire is there for you may find that the need to take that specific food out of your diet is merely to allow your emotional body to adapt to the vibratory change that is taking place within your aura. That is all.

We, Izaris, then, relate to you in terms of maintaining constitutional consistency. We wish to compare ourselves with the star Sirius. This is an important consciousness-form for your vessel as this is an energy he often brings through him in healing. If we look at the function of Sirius, it brings about a greater sense of cohesion or stickiness between the energy bodies within your auric being, so that as you evolve, you become more spiritually aware and have a greater sense of self. Often the displacement that takes place within your energetic environment, requires a little bit of glue to maintain a sense of cohesion. Sirius, in many ways, helps to bring this about, allowing you to maintain a greater sense of comfort-ableness as you, in your own way, experience your own healing with your own consciousness rising, thus giving you a greater ability to get on with life and be able to make coherent decisions. We, as Izaris, alter the charge within the cell by drawing on our energy but in doing so allow you to rebalance that constitutional nature of your being, which enables you to ascend to higher vibratory states of being in terms of consciousness-raising, in terms of greater understanding. Therefore your potential to acquire that becomes both real and effective. That is our purpose. That is our role.

Over the next ten weeks we are not about to move through every star within your galaxy and to explain its function and its purpose but we will make you more fully aware of your relationship with each. Each successive week is going to have a different context, taking a different aspect of your being and trying to elaborate and discuss it in a way that allows you to understand how it fits in with the stars that you see in your heavens. Izaris, as a star, as it exists in the heavens, has a physical place. There is an exact point where it exists. But it also has an exact point in a relation to time, so while you may look through a telescope at the star Izar, you are actually looking at a fixed point in time as you see it.

In 2000 years time, for example, we will not exist at this point in this way. We, as a consciousness-form, will have evolved to a different source within your physical universe, which in turn suggests that the star Izar will be placed differently within that physical universe. As this is true for us, this is also going to be true for every star that you have in your heavens. Looking at your solar system as it moves through space also means that the relationship, the physical relationship between your solar system and the stars in the heavens is going to be different from what you have now.

If you look at the Pyramids in Egypt, and if you look at the way those Pyramids have been constructed, and if you look at the passageways, not all of which have been found yet, and how they relate to the specific stars, there is information revealing the importance of certain stars and how they shine through these tunnels at certain periods. Do understand that what you have now is becoming very close to what was then when the Pyramids were first constructed. Their construction was more to do with creating a vibratory place on the earth to accelerate learning. So the stars that shine through the caverns of the Pyramids are extremely important as they relate to specific forms of consciousness. As society then was able to respond to that surge in consciousness-raising, there has to be a relationship. It isn't arbitrary. Deep within the Pyramid – it is difficult for us to describe verbally in mathematical form – there is a device that can explain the purpose of these particular stars. This device hasn't been found yet. Deep within the earth there is another device which can actually activate, almost like a crystal, further consciousness-raising at future times. As certain stars have had specific influence 3000 years ago – as you move into your next millennium – there are new stars that are going to activate these devices in a very different way, bringing forth a whole new understanding of consciousness that collectively the earth has not experienced before. These devices have been well hidden as there is no real sense of integrity about how these could be used in terms of the future yet, but that will become more apparent in the early years of the next millennium.

We are discussing this specifically for you to understand that, as there are cycles, there are also cycles within greater cycles, and that a cycle is coming to a close in terms of consciousness within the earth plane that is going to make a transformative leap into a new state of being. This you are already aware of. This you are already experiencing in terms of your own comfortableness as you seek your own truth, your own wisdom, your own peace; different vibratory states of being, we won't say new as they already exist, but different vibratory states of being. You then are the leaders of collective consciousness on the earth plane. This does not mean to say that you need to have elevated ideas about being great teachers. This is not required. In many ways your spiritual reality is withholding very specific teaching and information which is stimulating you within the human context to find that information inside yourselves. You live beside a well, the well dries up, there is no water. What do you do? Do you remain beside the well in the hope that it becomes wet again or do you seek some other place that may have water? The absence of water creates a motivation for you to look. The absence of teaching causes you to look inside yourself to find if you already have it. This is very important. Every individual within this room is already along that road, is already searching, has already had contact with a sense of their own truth and wisdom. So when we say that you lead, understand that your presence has a collective influence within the earth. We can go into greater detail about that but we believe that you already have a modicum of understanding of what it means.

What we have now in terms of your "earthliness" is the need to maintain physiological and emotional consistency, so that there is a sense of integration of the emotions that allows you to be an effective human being. In terms of the dissolution of structure within society, it means that you become examples, as you show what is possible by stepping outside belief, stepping outside received and organised thought and indoctrination, to demonstrate to others that by so doing you not only don't lose sight of who you are, you actually acquire greater insight of who you need to be. The conscious mind has difficulty entertaining what it needs, as what is needed is beyond your conceptualisation. To put yourself in a position where you can receive is important. Receive what, you don't know. That isn't important, that is not for you consciously to know, but for you to intuitively have an appreciation that there is something, that is important. What you need can create a spark within your being that takes away any effort in your relationship with life; that there is nothing to do here, there is nothing to aim for, there is nothing to achieve. Merely the experience of life in itself is enough. So the decisions that you worry about, that seem critical, in actuality are not – only that you have more room to manoeuvre, that there is much more flexibility that is more part of the life reality, more than you fully understand. Your vessel talks about freedom; mentally being prepared to let go of everything, but if there is nothing, there is no friction. If there is something, there is friction. If there is something to aim for, there is friction, and that friction creates a motivation to seek, to look and to understand. You seek enlightenment but does that mean that the chaos stops? Or does that mean that you are insightful enough to look through the chaos and experience it in a different way rather than the chaos stopping altogether? There has to be a sense of friction always. We are agreed there is no stillness. We are agreed there is only perpetual motion which means that your passage through time and space is relative and that you can only compare yourself to what you have at that moment. You can't compare it to what you had five minutes ago and you cannot equate it with what you will have tomorrow.

In very crude terms, time and space are part of the same thing. Space is your way to define time. Time is your means of measuring space. Intervals. You need to ask yourself the question: Is space merely a containment of time? And when you move into space it gives you a contained experience and within that space, there are very specific things for you to understand and experience. So, if we look at each life in a different space, if we look at the emotional, the spiritual and the cosmic as different spaces, you are very close to understanding the truth of the matter. Time can't be measured as it doesn't exist, as these are merely points on the graph that illustrate points of experience and learning. So time is irrelevant. I need to have enlightenment in my life. I need to achieve this or that in my life. This is almost a lie as your life is not one contained space. Your emotional experience of the human condition is a contained space. So that if you were to take all of your lives and put them together in one place and say, right, that is my experience of the human condition, that is one space, you would also place into that space the time between lives, so we are looking at the emotional-physical and the emotional-spiritual as one space, one time. You cannot look at time outside of that, as, from our perspective, it makes no sense. I don't have the time. Absolutely right, you don't have the time. It doesn't exist. You live within the milli-second of the breath of the universe, and that breath holds itself until you are able to move into the next space which is the next milli-second in terms of the breath within the universe. We stand observing this breath, this space, this time. We stand outside of this space, this time. We do not belong to it. We belong to a totally different context which is why it is often difficult for consciousness on our side of space to communicate within individuals of your side of space. As your space becomes more flexible, less limited, the potential for the emotional human to space-hop becomes greater; to move from context to context, to be able to receive different forms of consciousness. We mean this in terms of context more than anything else. As we seek to communicate in a very specific way for a very specific reason, so your ability to receive that for very specific reasons also increases through time. You enjoy the luxury at the moment of being able to have a sense of the accumulation of what is coming your way in terms of progress, in terms of importance, in terms of elevated thought. It is important that you look at what is possible rather than what is not. It is important that you work on the basis that anything is possible. Your need, particularly for those of you within this room, to be continually surprised, is vital. Try not to expect, as that may limit your experience of yourself and life. Allow things to happen. Allow things to be shown to you but do not expect them, as this restricts, in vibrational terms, your flexibility. Seek not to explain or justify, as that may invalidate your experience. Be open and allow your heart, in terms of your intuitive being, to appreciate the appropriateness of the experience, and what that may unlock in you at a future date.

We draw to a close this initial discourse. Merely reflect on your relationship to your physical and emotional state in the context of Izar. The influence that is coming from Izar is to bring flexibility into the densest state of your being. This is a preparatory stage. Our influence has never been felt on the earth before and it is here now to allow you to prepare yourselves for what you are about to become.

Are there any questions on what has been said ?

*Have you had contact with us before when we are asleep and is there some sort of manipulation above ourselves during our sleeping state taking place for the few months leading up to this evening?*

The sleeping state is when you are most vulnerable. The sleeping state is also when you are most flexible, when you are not tied down to a specific reality. Within your sleeping state, your ability to live, for simplicity's sake, in different dimensions at the same time, is great. The approach of our presence to earth has been accumulating over the last fifteen months. This is not anything that you would necessarily relate to in a specific way. Over the period of this calendar year, there has been a greater sense of, if you like, intrusion within structure, which may cause you to think or sense that there is a greater breakdown in conditioning, perception, than there has ever been before. This in some way is a contribution from us but it is also part of the organic growth in which you are involved that is acquiring an openness of understanding, that is relatively new and previously unexplored. To answer your question more specifically, yes. We do relate both consciously and unconsciously both within the sleep state and within the elevated mind as you allow yourself to meditate, commune or contemplate, as you allow your vibratory states to achieve resonances within higher degrees, or higher levels of understanding. Is there another question ?

*Are the crystal skulls which have been found related to the changes in consciousness ?*

Simply, no. The creators of the skulls are aware of a certain magnetic power that they can have that can alter people's perceptions. For those who come in contact with these skulls there can be a magnification and this magnification can create, in simple terms, a sensitivity. This sensitivity is important because it alerts people to what is possible. It makes them less defensive. The emanation of energy from these skulls is quite powerful but to revert to your question, the answer is no.

*I have a question about meditation. About two months ago I had this sensation of blue light where I almost came to nothing. Any insight ?*

There is an establishment with your own creativity. If we look at your creativity as what you are, the sense of reticence that has been associated with your communicating to others and to yourself in the past – as that dissolves – what you experience is an intensity of your own being. As you move and develop, what you experience is a greater sense of you. The intensity of what you experience is in fact you, but you without boundary, without physical boundary, without spiritual boundary. It relates purely to your own creative source.

*I have a question: Is it possible to move beyond the emotional or spiritual beings and still operate comfortably or indeed effectively in the human state ?*

Yes. You know that well and you see that more often than you think. This will be discussed later on in greater depth. We will bring to a conclusion the first sitting. Do not feel your need to remember, merely reflect on what the sense of this coming together means. This will establish within you a sense of your own progressive nature and where that will possibly lead.

Take a moment to focus on your heart. Try and get a sense

of the inter-connection of all the hearts in the room, so that you become one heart. Relate that to your vessel, the speaker. Try and get a sense of what that is in vibrational terms without the need to define it. For the space, we are grateful, and your presence, we respect. Until the next time.

# TWO

## *Movement and Motion*

As we enfold our vessel within our light, focus on the peace within your own heart. Within the context of this evening's discussion, we will concentrate mainly on movement and motion; motion in terms of planetary motion, movement in terms of consciousness, energy and emotional development.

As we look physically at the solar system, at the heavens, there is a certain synchronicity of movement that never exactly repeats itself even though certain planetary aspects relate in similar and not disproportional ways to the earth as they have before. This allows the human on the earth, as an emotional being, to establish a sense of belonging within the continuity of movement and consciousness, both in terms of energy support, and in terms of your own personal and psychological development. As the planets orbit around the sun they never align themselves exactly in the same way twice. As the solar system moves through the universe and as the stars align themselves to the configuration of the planets within the solar system, even though they may be perceived geometrically at certain angles, we do not have an exact repetition of their alignment. What you see are specific planets, specific stars coming into view in a particular way so that they can be perceived in terms of north, south, east and west, with a certain exactness that seems to repeat itself. However, the further out you go into the heavens, in terms of angle of degree, it means that there is never the exact same degree or relationship to the earth plane. In terms of consciousness, these stars have a particular resonance that draws to them certain consciousness forms within certain contexts. So understand that their degree or relationship to earth means that their influence will either be greater or lesser. Also understand that the information will be given in a different way and received in a different way, so that not only your perception of us, but our perception of you, will be different, as the information is also different.

As you look down a canal with many different bridges, or locks, it means sometimes some of the locks are closed and some are open, and as we move through time, figuratively speaking, more and more of the locks are being opened, so not only is there greater availability of information, there is also greater accessibility for you. This is such an important point to remember, because in terms of your own evolutionary development, it means, in a totally illogical way, that you are able to recognise more and more what is possible, and your ability to concentrate on that as a progressive element of your being becomes greatly enhanced, rather than your need to look at what is not possible, or that you are part of some sort of regression, in terms of evolution. This will gradually slow down to such a degree that no longer will you pay any attention to it. It is important that you look at this very special, or peculiar, time in which you live, and are able to see equally the possibilities as well as the restrictive movement.

That is why many of you view the earth as being in a peculiar state of balance or imbalance, where the ability to heal and grow, or to evolve and destroy, are both possible. You don't have to concern yourself with the possibility of ultimate destruction. Your concern only is with your own personal development, and this is not meant in an exclusive or selfish way. As the personal becomes more flexible in its attitude and perception, you can then relate it more easily to the Grand Plan: being able to look more at the possibility of what is happening; be able to have insight into the reason why things are progressing as they are. It is not until you can see the way things are working as they are, mechanically, that you can make a quantum leap in terms of understanding, and evaluate them in greater terms. Rather than feel that there is something destructive at work within your earth that is going to bring about its demise, you can actually see at a superficial level why there is a degree of destruction and demise within your society, which won't be total. So that you can recognise the destruction but you can understand why there is a need to burn away the belief that inhibits, to allow what doesn't inhibit to grow and flourish.

What you will see are many disasters. What you will experience is a breakdown of the habitual nature of the economic society as you have it, as it will no longer habitually support itself as it has been used to. Your own psychological movement suggests that as there is greater access to higher sources or more developed forms of consciousness, it will require every one of you to allow your own psychological make-up to become flexible. This means that, within the next fifty years, what you experience emotionally within the context of your society, will be total breakdown of order. So those who rule, in the political sense of the word, are going to have to become very inventive indeed in terms of their approach. No longer are people going to be able to be pacified by forms of expression, by jingoism. Everybody, with a broad sweep of the brush, is becoming more intelligent. There are degrees within this and this intelligence merely means that people, more and more, are able to appreciate both sides of an argument without having to come down in favour of either. This allows the individual, by being intelligent, to weigh up what is the most appropriate way to proceed.

Change, as you understand it, is going to happen at such a rapid rate, that there will be no formal set plan because no formal set plan is going to last very long. As to length of time, we would estimate any plan instigated during the next half-century would last for about four years. After that, that particular plan would be largely redundant. For any political or dogmatic philosophy to sustain itself, there is a need continually to have insight, to anticipate change, to anticipate mood, to anticipate need. So that we can actually embrace the plan within society, the plan within your emotional being, and the need, in terms of your own spiritual understanding.

As you respond less to expectations, it allows you to respond more to what you have at every given moment. This makes it difficult, then, to plan any group behaviour long term. And you will notice, particularly over the next fifteen years, that any established group that sets out any formalised ethos or objectives, will find it very difficult to hold to these, as those objectives will be virtually unobtainable. If that sort of change is required within a fifteen year period, allow yourself to appreciate what that will mean within a fifty year period if we have an accumulation of speed, and there is momentum gathering here that is going to motivate in a particular way, which may mean that the four year plans of the next fifty years may only take nine months to a year. We are helpless, we hear you ask. Maybe you are, but do you feel that you are victims? If you don't feel that you are victims, you respond, because you instinctively know that you are in command but that there is no need to control. If you feel that you need to control, you have a problem because it will suggest that you are not flexible enough to adapt, which will mean, yes, you are helpless.

So what will you do? Not all of you will be present in fifty years. This is nothing to do with anything fundamental. We merely try to give an indication of the sort of rapidity to come, and how the intuitive and psychological make-up will have to adapt. It relates purely to the personal. You are already experiencing the need to let go, so that you don't hang on to specific paramaters. If you believe in your circumstances enough, it means that the belief won't allow you to believe anything else. That is where the fundamental difficulty lies. That is where the difficulty within society, as it exists for you now, lies. Because there isn't a concept of freedom. We don't mean this necessarily in terms of ultimate freedom, being free from everything, but having the power to use your time not given over to work or formalised activity freely. Whatever time you have left for you, you have the freedom to use this time as you see fit, and in the rewards which come from that, no matter how superficial they are, is where your freedom lies.

The alignment of particular stars, as they are in terms of their own cycle, coming into prominence once more within your reality, means that what created wisdom on earth 3-4,000 years ago – conscious wisdom – those particular stars are aligning themselves in a not dissimilar position again, to make that wisdom doubly powerful and influential. We talked in our last discourse about the planetary aspects influencing the Pyramids in Egypt. As they come round for a second time, we have an intensification of an accelerated learning period. This accelerated learning period, in your time, is going to last approximately 1700 – 2000 years. After this period, those stars are going to leave the universe as you see it now, and there is going to be a rearrangement within the physical universe that will show itself in a completely fresh way. What your astronomers will see are very old stars, older than the universe, that they have never seen before. How can that be? How can there be stars present within the universe that are actually older than the universe itself? Is it possible that there is wisdom beyond what you already know, which can show itself in a way, when the time is right, that can allow the human race to evolve at a more rapid rate than it can possibly anticipate or imagine? Is it possible for a young universe to hold within it old stars? This is an argument that scientists are going to take many decades not only to come to terms with but also to understand. Their approach to the whole physical system of the universe is infinitesimally narrow. What they understand is only limited to what they can see. Consequently, the hypotheses that are postulated are largely inaccurate, as they cannot possibly comprehend the enormity of the cycles of activity that are taking place as universe upon universe dovetails with each universe that approximates its own position. As we relate these universes to different consciousnesses, what you have as a race to understand, within these universe existences, is: What does our race need to learn and understand? Do we reach a point when there is nothing for us to understand any more? If that is so, and we say it is so, then what is left for your race? Science already understands that there is no stillness. Science already understands that dynamic instability cannot contain itself. So there has to be a quantum leap, not only in terms of understanding, but also in terms of energy state of being, so that your race, as it exists now, when there is nothing left to learn, will experience a catalytic catharsis which will allow it to make that leap into a new state of being, which will bring you directly into a new universe. This is fact. This is very real. Though this isn't something necessarily that you can entertain, try to understand the principle. There are already stars within your universe that are older than your universe. Ask yourself the question then: What does that mean? There are beings on the earth, there are consciousness-forms contained within beings on the earth, that are older than time itself. What does that mean to you? We are not being enigmatic. We merely wish you to reflect on the question so that you can understand the implications.

There is less and less of a sense of the arbitrariness within your universe as science understands the interconnectedness more and more; the way that the universe is composed. Science is already aware of the worm holes that move through the universe. These worm holes, or vacuums of energy that move through time and space, connect different paths of space physically, for no particular reason. Do not relate these to anything such as black holes that are created by the implosion of stars. These worm holes are merely mechanisms that allow consciousness to move through space without being confined by time or position. Again, remember what we said in our last discussion about the nature of time and space. We refresh your memory that time is very much more to do with position than duration, and so when we relate time to your physical universe, we talk about position more than duration. That you are in a particular position to experience something very specific. Once your understanding of that specific nature is complete, then you can move on to a different position. That is an over-simplification of what we wish to say, but it is very close to what we mean.

Your emotions and your feelings, which in many ways are the densest part of your being, are greatly accepted by this inter-connectedness of space, and as this is very highly lubricated, it moves. It moves over itself, within itself, and there are dimensions within it. And as those dimensions literally shift their position, as they blend with each other, this does cause, in terms of your emotional being, friction, and you can't explain this. You can't justify what you can't see, what you can't understand. Your vessel talks about living outside the box, that is, you don't know what exists outside the box until you experience what is there. But that doesn't mean to say there isn't anything beyond what you have already experienced. How can you invite into your life, how can you allow yourself to be alert to, that which you don't already understand or comprehend can even exist? You can't. You have to wait for it to reveal itself to you. You have to wait for it to impose itself, not in an invasive way, but in a way that allows you to become alert. Once you are alert, then possibility is a very great reality.

Within your emotional being there are dense clouds of energy that represent your personality and character. For simplicity's sake, please don't take this too literally. They relate in the way that fingerprints relate to physical identification. These emotional clouds are unique to every individual. These clouds begin to evaporate. They are in the sun, and the sun causes the water vapour to dissipate and dissolve, so that your emotional being becomes stretched. You become aware of your strength. How? Through becoming more vulnerable and more sensitive. So within the context of your society, there are many people who are not only looking within themselves at who they are, they are also looking for verification within those people and situations that they have around them. They can't always find out about themselves by doing this. It creates anxiety and it creates a re-trenching within what they already believe. There are those – and the people we are about to speak of now are gathering momentum – who are able to look beyond the need to identify, who, when they look within themselves, have a sense of a greater being. Of themselves being part of something much wider and all-embracing and, like a boat going across the water, it allows them to skim over that surface of superficiality, which you call life.

As these clouds evaporate, they leave you free from restriction. You then have to decide: Do I want to be restricted or not? Can I live without the need to feel secure? Or can I embrace something much wider that gives me security of being in a way that I can't justify or logically come to terms with ? And can I allow myself to embrace that without any form of anxiety, knowing that I, meaning you, am part of something that is naturally evolving and unfolding and belong to it in such an intimate way that, of course, it is supportive. Of course, it is loving. And of course, if you wish to be that open, it will lead you where you need to be, and of that you have no prior knowledge or experience. You merely have a sense of appropriateness, and you daren't look at that too closely, because that illogicality evokes fear of beingness itself. So the question, or the conundrum, is: Can I live a life in a circumstance over which I have no ultimate understanding, but somewhere within myself, there is a sense of completeness and security of being that somehow allows me to entertain in no matter how small a way, that possibility exactly?

In terms of healing, and that ever-growing number of people, who are coming to not only understand what that means but to use it, this means that there are many, now, who can give assistance to those who feel, in your language, out of balance. What are they doing? They are bringing the psychology and the emotional state into some form of stability. There are other healers who are activating or awakening the consciousness within so that it becomes more conscious. So that actually people become what they need to be. This isn't about change. This is about progression. You need to understand the word change. As all is, there is a certain consistency, a web, an energetic web, that supports all that is. So there are already channels that connect everything to everything. What you experience in terms of life is that journey towards experiencing all. This doesn't necessarily involve change, but it reflects a progressive being becoming something else. You may see that in a limited sense of change. We are being rather pedantic to make you aware of the nature of reality in terms of its progression rather than it having to become something else. As there is no 'have to', it is more a question of 'it is already required and will happen'. The way that you perceive it and relate to it is something entirely different. Already, your psychologists, your psychiatrists, are becoming aware of the limitations of pure analysis; of looking at the subjective conscious in clinical, cut and dried terms. It has reached a point now where, virtually, there is nothing further to explore. Human nature is human nature. Human nature as it is evolving becomes something more. Your analysis of it, however, is merely a superficial device to understand it purely at a superficial level. That is restrictive. It is dead. It doesn't go anywhere. There are many people, now, who are beginning to develop their work in such a manner to allow them to relate emotionally to people, psychologically to people, in a way that they can't always define; that isn't defined by specific teaching or learning patterns. These are the people who are becoming aware of the need to work for the individual as the individual presents him or herself, rather than feeling that the individual has to fit in to particular patterns. The idea, therefore, within psychotherapeutic terms, of the archetype, is totally redundant. Human nature as it is evolving, particularly now, can really no longer fit in to that shallow mould. The need to look beyond the mould to what causes the mould to happen in the first place is far more productive. As you have an energy body surrounding you which creates the physical body, understand that there is something beyond the energy body, a blueprint within which this totality actually fits. So it is, with your psychology and your emotional being. So, also, it is with your spiritual being, because understand that this is part of the same context. We don't wish to speak at length about that today as it is something we will talk about in greater depth later.

Do understand that your emotional being has reached a point when it really can't sustain itself any more as it did. So the habitual sense of being, belonging and doing, is at an end. Not for everyone, but in terms of a marker, in time, it is an end. As you move through time, over many hundreds and thousands of years, there will be a separation within your solar system of the planets as they revolve around your sun. It will become less compact. There will be greater distance between each. This is a preparatory state towards making a leap into this new state of being that we were talking about earlier. When this gravitational force begins to theoretically dissolve, the earth moves away from the sun, which totally changes the atmosphere around the planet, which means, physiologically, your ability to utilise energy in a whole different capacity becomes very necessary. This, then, is the time when the molecules you have within your body separate to such a degree that you no longer need to hold on to a physical state. The body will begin to glow, and rather than the molecules and cells of the body having a sense of density, there will be energy bridges which will create or maintain form beyond matter. You will maintain a shape without density. The physiological functions within the body will no longer operate in the same way. Your ability to draw nourishment from your environment, from the air that you have around you, will increase. Almost as a fish respires within water, so you will respire within air. Your need to nourish yourself will not be with food but with other energy forms. Not only will you, as individuals, become these glowing beings, all life on earth will adapt in the same way. There will be less form in terms of flora. There will be some form in terms of fauna. The earth will remain merely as a magnet and this will create a different relationship of human to earth as it exists now, for you will no longer rely on it in the same way. It, as a living organism, will have less to teach you. This, then, will become a preparatory state to allow the human individual to move more freely through time and space. Your position, then, going back to time in terms of position, the position and the potential for that position to move, will become very real. This is when those very old stars within the young universe, can guide you to a new place; as indicated by the sine curve, the sine curve relating to the creation of matter, and the sine curve as it goes into anti-matter, which, at the moment, your scientists perceive as the "big crash" or the "big crunch", where matter, or your universe as you understand it, can no longer sustain itself. They are right inasmuch as it will become something else. They are wrong in perceiving it as a destruction. As we see it, there is a natural evolution, not necessarily into an anti-matter state, but into another matter state, which doesn't have density attached to it. This is the point when you totally lose your emotional being. So your relationship then, to your spiritual reality, becomes very different indeed.

We stop at that point in terms of this relationship between emotional matter and spiritual matter. Just be aware, for the moment, of the nature of this progression. Again, putting this in context with the different universes as they accumulate throughout all space and relate this microcosm of what we would term banality, and look at this microcosm in terms of the macrocosm, because the analogy, the picture, the telescopic vision, is not that dissimilar when you project that out into physical space. Allow yourself to dwell on the vision and allow yourself to allow that stillness within your heart to make you aware, consciously, of the psychic pictures that are shown as you see within. These pictures will allow you to reflect not only on your own nature, your own beingness, but they will also allow you to conceive more of the possibility of what is. We can only see, or contemplate, what is potentially within our ability to conceptualise. We see a bigger picture but again, we, within the context of our being, are also limited. That is the way that it is. This limitation as we explained earlier to some degree creates a sense of friction, that creates a motivation to understand and explore. That is all.

Are there any questions ?

*Is the theory of the universe being a hologram an accurate represen-tation of the universe ?*

From your perspective, yes. If you look at the hologram as

having no density, of there really being no rationale to time, space and matter, yes. This is the most accurate analogy that you can make, but understand that the hologram is also a limiting concept. If, once you become the hologram, there is also a super-hologram which totally redefines what a hologram represents, then you are closer to the truth. If you find chess demanding, make it three-dimensional, make it four-dimensional, make it five-dimensional. There is always something else that you can add on. So in many ways, what we are trying to say is that the hologram, while being useful, is, from it's own perspective, limiting. But as a device to aid under-standing, yes. As far as your universe is concerned, it is not a bad example to use. Is there another question?

*Are we being prepared for this lesson, because I found this time and last time most of the things you are talking about I have thought about three or four days previously? Actually it has occupied my mind quite a great deal.*

Understand first that in our composition we have never spoken before. In terms of being aware of what is being said, we see our role as trying to emotionalise what we see. We try to relate that to your own emotional perception. We don't have this perception but as we throw a cloak, an energy cloak, around this group, it creates a certain resonance that may give you some precognitive recognition. If you are perceiving that before it happens, you are merely perceiving the energy cloak that is already thrown around this group. If you regard this cloak as a geometric net that is very exact, you live within this net day by day, even when you aren't present in this building, and you are susceptible to what is contained within it. This is a device to allow you to be able to contain more of the concepts, it is also to introduce you to this quality of energy-being that is largely held by your vessel, and this allows you in turn to emotionally relate to what is being said more. Is that understood ?

*Thank you very much, yes.*

Is there another question ?

*Yes there is, but I'm not sure that I can articulate it properly. We set out a structure of indoctrination and we go into living and being and you say this is freedom. I am presently in that position. I don't feel comfortable, this is new to me. Presumably this is what I'm meant to be doing at the moment. It is actually doing , being. Does that make sense? Learning to be ?*

You relinquished your hold on your physical reality as it became too uncomfortable. What allowed you to do that was your sense of there being something else, or something greater, that drew you to it. That doesn't necessarily mean that you step outside of living. It brings you to a point when you reach a state of being that is relative to nothing except yourself When you feel you can give yourself permission to be, to be what? To be ordinary? To introduce yourself into society again? But with a fuller vision of what that means. What all of you are looking for is permission to be. Permission to fail. Permission to explore. Permission to understand. Without feeling that you have to do anything with this being or understanding. To do that, it often needs or requires that you have to put yourself in a position where, for you, it seems that nothing is happening. Where there is total inactivity. Where you have no work. Where you have no occupation. Life is about extremes. The understanding of life brings you to a point when you don't have to live those extremes. That is the only purpose of life. Reaching a point where there is no struggle. Then, your need to be part of life, in the physical sense of the word, is redundant. Reaching the point when you need no longer challenge yourself in this way, gives you ultimate freedom. Does that answer your question?

*Yes it does. Thank you very much.*

Is there another?

*Yes. Have people in the past made some sort of a quantum leap, for example the Mayans?*

There are beings who approach the earth plane, and as they come close to the earth plane, they understand the meaning of life and immediately leave before coming into the physical body. There are those, in the physical sense of the word, who are very old indeed, in your terms, who have been around for many centuries, who seek to live and experience the meaning of life without death. And there are those who do make that quantum leap. There are those who carry within them – this is difficult for us to describe – a double-being, where they are composed of not only their own personality-essence, but take on board the personality-essence of other consciousness forms. This is nothing to do with possession. Don't take this description too literally, it's a bit like soul-sharing within the body; you share your body with another consciousness-form. That gives you proportionately accelerated learning as a gift for allowing that consciousness form to experience physical being. All things are possible. You do not recognise, you do not see these individuals as they are. That is how it is meant to be. Some can. Some do.

Mostly, you do not. As long as you allow yourself to understand that there is more form to life than you see. Is there another question ?

*Why are you giving us this information now? For our time and space it seems far too advanced for this group. I mean it will not happen within our time frame and this ordinary reality that we are experiencing. Or, is there another level on which we shall experience this, either in our future or in a parallel reality, particularly now ?*

You do yourself a great injustice by saying that. How can the flower anticipate day before it comes, or have a sense of night before it arrives? Why do you take on physical bodies to experience life, when all you feel you experience is frustration and pain? Why do you question yourselves so much with this pain and anxiety when all you require is joy, love and the need to be free? Do you perhaps need to compare more to understand? This information is not new. This information has been around for many thousands of years. The surfacing of this information through the voice of another makes you aware, in theory, of what is possible. Do not underestimate the multi-dimensional nature of your being. Do not underestimate that there are other aspects of consciousness relative to you in existence now. Do not underestimate, as you term it, your higher self being able to absorb this information, and to inject this into your being in such a way that it is never forgotten, and that it is actually totally assimilated. Do not forget to remember that life is about experience, and all experience is accumulative and is never lost, and as you move through time and space, you draw on the reservoir of that experience to support not only what you already know but to give you a sense of security –

of being able to support – that which you don't know. It leaves you in a perpetual state of: 'I don't know what is happening'. It leaves you in a perpetual state of: 'I don't know what I need'. This doesn't mean that you won't be given what you need, and this doesn't mean to say you won't experience understanding. What it only means is somehow, in some extraordinary way, you come to experience the totality of being, the more you allow yourself to look outside the box. Look outside the box. Be alert and allow yourself to receive. You don't know what you're looking for but, as your intuition and instinct becomes sharper, you will be able to recognise truth, progression, eventually all, without ever possibly having that final vision. But then, as we have already explained, that final vision is the motivation to existence. Period.

We wish to draw this discourse to a close now. Again, just register the peace within your heart for a moment. Maintain your own harmony within what you sense, within what you feel. Allow yourself to be open and truthful by acknowledging what you sense and what you feel. Do not put pressure on yourselves by thinking, 'I have to'. By merely acknowledging and being truthful, you're just admitting to what you are. And let it be. Until the next time.

# THREE

## *Music and Sound*

The focus of our communication this evening is music and the reverberation of this sphere of consciousness that pervades the universe. Your vessel often talks about what he calls the harmonic; that emanation of light that comes from the Source, of which the physical body is an expression, within which there is an accumulation of colour, light and sound which is a representation of everything about that individual. This harmonic has a direction, a trajectory that moves through space, which gives that individual, as a consciousness-form, not only a perspective but a context in terms of living, and in terms of being. The colour is self-explanatory, the light is the degree of intensity and the sound is connected to the mathematical configuration, or the fingerprint that is unique for every human being. Because of the density human beings possess, in terms of your presence on earth, there is little flexibility of how that sound can develop, and there is a very particular line of experience which you have to endure to allow yourselves to gain understanding of life and reality. When we move away from the dense physicality of the human body we come into different spheres of being that allow all of us to enter into what you would call higher forms of consciousness. It is this sound that becomes, from our perspective, very important in terms of communication, both of what is possible for you to have access to and understand, as well as what you cannot, as it is not part of your learning curve as human beings. As you begin to appreciate the vibratory nature of your being beyond the physical, it activates the harmonic in a particular way.

As you look at the piano, you regard the centre of the piano as middle C. As you acknowledge your vibratory being beyond the physical, you begin to experience the C above and the C below. Depending on how sophisticated your understanding is of what is beyond the physical, you begin to understand the cause within the notes that define the parameters of your existence. For example, your notes may be contained within the C below middle C and the C above, and everything between that is to do with your reality. It may be you only have one note either side of middle C which means that your ability to appreciate or to understand consciousness is far more limited. So in your terms your being able to access the harmony within those notes becomes much reduced. This is how it is. There are those of you who have that potential and those of you who don't, depending on what you set out to learn through your emotional experience of life and also of the spiritual reality; not forgetting that the spiritual reality is very much a reflection of your emotional being in a different state.

The trajectory of the harmonic, like a beam of light that shines from the earth into space, like a laser beam that goes on for infinity, has particular mapping properties which takes it through certain planets as, at that moment in time, they have configurations which will cause you to feel and experience different aspects of your psychological and emotional condition. As that beam of light moves beyond the solar system into your galaxy, there is a greater sense of stability so that as that beam of light moves along its particular trajectory, your experience of yourself coming closer to the blueprint of what you actually are becomes more stable and more fundamental. As you move outside that galaxy with which you are familiar, you move into a whole different area of comprehension of which there is no prior knowledge or prior sense. That doesn't mean to say that this does not exist, nor does it mean that you are beyond being influenced by it, depending on whatever evolutionary point you happen to be at. So when we look in your galaxy at the formation of energy, of consciousness, of life, if you wish, depending on that line of trajectory, it will mean, in terms of your blueprint, that there are certain qualities, aspects, indeed wisdom, which will seek to assert itself within each lifetime. This is so much part of your eternal being that there is, from your perspective, no choice as to what influence comes from this blueprint. But again you must understand a fundamental tenet here. It is only by virtue of your emotional development and by you acquiring emotional stability that you can look within the galaxy itself for information. Once you have that stability, then your potential to absorb whatever your harmonic is allowed to attract to it, becomes great. For example, if what you need to understand are particular aspects of manipulation and control, then, as that trajectory passes through your solar system, it will experience emotional fluctuations as you try to understand how much you need to control and how much you can let go of control. As you move out more into the stars within the galaxy, it allows you to understand what you are sacrificing, in terms of wisdom and understanding, by controlling, and how much you are allowing yourself to be directed by letting go of the need to control. As you move that trajectory beyond the familiarity of your trajectory, the element of control no longer exists. But what we have is an expansion of that restriction into a whole different state of being which brings about not only the whole destruction of control itself but its very existence, which takes us into the dimension of needing to perpetuate continuation of matter.

At an emotional level, therefore, you may be working at a level of control beyond your galaxy. Or, the aspect of your being, as it exists there, is relating to you in terms of: Do I need my consciousness to be contained within matter to gain further understanding, or can I allow myself to move outside the nature of matter itself to gain understanding? At a human level, this may make no logical sense as there is no emotional empathy with what we are saying. From our perspective there is a very great understanding of the nature of matter and non-matter, and indeed, anti-matter, which is really consciousness existing in a position – not a time but a position – where we explore everything beyond the need to contain, and that is our purpose. Understand the three different realities which are crudely presented to you and allow yourself to relate to them in whatever way you feel is most appropriate.

Let's look at what is embracing this trajectory, this harmonic. We have different energy forms, different spheres of light, different consciousness-representations. Each of these representations has within it spheres of sound. Within your galaxy these sounds are composite. They are composed of many different vibrations. Each sound, each note, has a purity, an essence of truth that can be communicated, so that when an accumulation of these essences is brought together, we have a versatility and a subtlety, a complexity that can be conveyed. But also understand that within each note there are further sub-divisions, and within the sub-divisions there is even greater refinement. That is not only beyond your auditory capacity to experience but is also beyond your scientific means to measure. But within science there is an awareness of these sub-divisions.

The property, or quality, that sound has, is to create an alertness. That is all. That alertness has a context. You may see it as a database. There is information contained within this context. So that as you become alert to sound, not only are you becoming alert to the nature of your trajectory through time and space, you are also being made alert to the context, the information, that relates to that point in time and space. Many of you might perceive this as an aspect of philosophical understanding. This philosophical understanding allows you to put what you sense into an area of containment where it makes greater sense. It allows you to bring a sense of familiarity to that which is not familiar. You experience this alertness, even though you may not understand what you are being made alert to (because you haven't experienced it before) and so there is nothing to which you can relate it until you have a further experience within this context. It doesn't mean to say that this context doesn't exist. You always have a need for proof and justification, even though when you think you don't, you do. And there is always that little voice inside your mind that wants someone or something to say: Believe what you understand, believe what you know. And what you find frustrating is that the little voice never does come along and say: Believe what you know and what you understand. Because you never can.

You don't have the clarity. But there is that little irritant within your heart that continues, no matter how insecure you may feel in relation to what you experience beyond your conscious perception. It pushes you a little further, which causes you to experience something else beyond your limits of perception. So that over a period of time, collectively, you have a group experience which somehow makes sense at the level that you experience it. You then reach a point when you can no longer ignore what this experience means. There is difficulty in making this logical, but do understand the premise.

At the level at which you are used to communicating, which is the emotional, we have great density. At the level of your experience, there isn't the density in the emotional context, so that you can't relate to it emotionally, which is exactly why there is this form of communication. Because we come from a realm of existence where there is no feeling and emotion as you experience it, that doesn't mean to say that we don't exist collectively as a consciousness-form, not, we hasten to add, as a personality essence, because that requires emotion and feeling, and we don't have that. Higher consciousness does not have that. There is no personality within higher consciousness so immediately you have to lose the need to identify and to define, because this is not possible. We can't stress this enough.

What is your Source? Where does it come from? How can you believe that your Source and teaching is wise and truthful? You can't ever know except to understand the effect that any particular received wisdom has on you. If it causes some shift in your understanding, even if that shift is to consolidate what you already know, then you can register whether that form of communication is real or not, enlightened or not. We do not ask to be believed. We merely wish for what is being communicated to be entertained, to be conceptualised. There is no need to contain what is said here. There is no need to make it into anything. There is no need to define what we say in emotional terms. It is being given in a way that can allow you to have a degree of emotional relationship with it. That is important, and the reason this whole information is being given in the first place is to allow you to have a degree of identification so you can appreciate your own movement.

Returning to these spheres of music that embrace the harmonic; you will come in contact with a very specific vibratory force depending on your trajectory. These musical spheres have very specific relationships to you, as you need them. Within the context of your seen galaxy, they mostly allow you to understand limitation and their purpose is to be able to take you beyond that containment. That is all. So if we look at your solar system and then at your galaxy we have an experience of restriction. Then we have an understanding of the restriction which allows you to be free from it altogether. Sound, music, activates within your cerebral cortex, a memory that actually isn't conscious, but is contained within your consciousness nevertheless. That alerts you to your harmonic. What we are saying in more simple terms, is that sound alerts you to your direction, to your path, to your purpose, to your destiny. You may not be consciously aware of what it is, but that alertness happens nevertheless. When you look at music within the emotional context – how you experience that on a day-to-day basis – when you examine the quality of that music, it is actually indicative of that group's cultural belief and what it needs to experience. And when you examine the musicality, more in your terminology than ours, of that expression, it allows you to understand the complex nature of that reality. When you examine the great composers, where music relates more to harmony (or actually, in a very deliberate way, moving against harmony) you can understand the convoluted nature of how your society is evolving, both in your perception in terms of the Western world and the Eastern world, in terms of the northern and southern hemispheres, and in terms of the closed societies and those societies which are open to others' influences.

Through medieval times you have a sense of the purity of the note, an experiencing of the note that is almost sacred. During the age of the Reformation, the note is expanded and there is an experience of harmony, of complexity, of notes coming together in greater quantities, which create compositions of musicality that haven't previously existed. Coming closer to this present century and certainly moving through this present century, there is a harshness, a cacophony that enters music, which is unpleasant to some and not to others. Almost to the point where there is a complete polarisation in terms of musicality and in terms of harmony, musical harmony, and the harmonics that are stimulated within that harmony. And this music, in many ways, reflects the society or the cultural aspects to which you belong. Within open societies, by that we mean those who have access to other cultures, other societies, that cacophony is becoming greater. There is a grating here. There is an uncomfortableness. Within those societies which are closed, there is a greater sense of musicality, of harmony, as that culture exists for itself. This is important to remember. So at a very basic, mundane level, your music is reflective of your own emotional and psychological states. As you look for sound, you may not always know what you are looking for, but when you hear it, you recognise sound for the quality it brings into your life because it is a quality that is needed in terms of your balance and your growth, if you are looking at life in that particular way. If you are not, you look for those sounds that deny your existence. As those sounds on their trajectory permeate and extend into space, those spheres of music which are attracted to that individual, will merely reflect the individual's needs. If this is to increase, and thereby create a greater disturbance in the learning process, so be it. If the need being projected is to bring about balance and harmony and peace, that is what will be attracted to that particular harmony. There is no conscious understanding of this, but within the cerebral cortex, what is activated is virtually a chemical composite that runs and rushes through the body, which communicates almost at a primeval physio-logical level, an experience that is vital to the human condition. You may not listen to music often, even though you are yourself music. The need for silence is often to hear clearly what you are, and within this, there is sound. Consciously, you may not hear this. Consciously, you may. But to create an alertness where your attention is diverted in that way, is very important.

What is the purpose of old stars within a new universe? If there is a certain wisdom and stability attached to these old stars, which regulate – and we do stress this word – experience, it takes the intensity of pain away. So as your consciousness experiences itself within your galaxy, it allows you to create understanding without emotional pain. So the more you allow yourself to rise above your emotional situation, and as you experience yourselves doing this, you may sometimes feel yourself being very deliberately able to move in and out of pain. In and out of grief. In and out of joy. Choosing to do it very deliberately. Please understand, this is you moving your vibratory scale up and down from the galaxy to the solar system, from the solar system to the galaxy. This is part of your commitment to yourselves to experience life and be a part of it. This is why you are here, like it or not. But what is happening to consciousness as it exists on the earth now is being able to experience more and more the context of what is contained within the galaxy rather than what is contained within the solar system. The sound which is emanating from the galaxy has a certain magnetism that draws your consciousness to it. You experience choices like: Do I fundamentally want to experience the free nature of my being? If you do, you allow yourself to be drawn up to that higher aspect of being. If you do not, or once you have experienced it, if that creates too much of a loosening of constriction or restriction, you go back to experiencing yourself within the solar context. This is the point of your evolutionary development. Some of you now are making that leap from the solar system to the galaxy, but there are others who feel they can't, because their notion of freedom is so great that it creates too much that is unknown for them to contain, not understanding that that containment doesn't exist.

The music, which can be defined mathematically, creates an aura around your solar system. Not around your earth, but around your solar system. And this aura, not to be confused with your own emotional being, has certain protective qualities that act as a buffer to what is beyond it. And the more that people activate this level of consciousness by entering into it, the greater flexibility is created within this particular strata of being, and it becomes more porous, allowing energy, understanding or consciousness from beyond this strata to permeate through this level of being, so eventually it can interact with the consciousness which is the solar system itself. At the moment, the strata of being that is acting as a buffer is very slowly breaking down. So, very deliberately and with great precision, there are tiny holes of light coming through from beyond this strata of objectivity. Let us call this super-objectivity. And as we go into this super-objectivity, we become closer to the essence of being, and in many ways, this is what you are reaching for. This is that which you are trying to have access to. This isn't the ultimate, but in terms of your own emotional and spiritual development, this is the reality. This is sense and this is the wisdom. This is realised being. Realised being and a notion of matter. Hold that in your minds. To become realised means that there is a complete understanding of matter. The ability to manipulate matter. The need, or not as the case may be, to sustain yourself within matter is completely understood. That is the point when you no longer have need for the physical body. This is what the Buddhists aspire to. Already the Buddhists, by virtue of their existence collectively as a consciousness force, have an understanding of the nature of being, of physical being, as it relates to consciousness, which no other grouping on the earth has, and this is important. There is a consciousness-grouping within South America who understand the nature of spiritual development and where that is heading in terms of individuals, society and the earth itself. Western society is caught up in a mechanism of experiencing change – by your definition change – and acts as a living example of what is possible and what is not. What we can do and what we can't. How we succeed and how we fail. Recognise your own part in that. You are suspended between two magnets, and it is those two magnets which allow sustained being. When the energy is no longer present in those magnets, you no longer have physical being. There is no need for consciousness to experience the conditional life further.

The nature of the chant, no matter what belief is

associated with it, brings people to an experience of themselves, releases them into an area of consciousness within themselves that takes them beyond while still being present in the physical body. It is not what you should chant for, you can't chant for anything. At least you can, but that doesn't mean to say that that is what you will receive. Chanting amplifies your being. It brings you into an experience of yourself which is terribly physical and very, very real, but do understand, it activates the higher echelon of your emotional experience of being, be that physical or spiritual. It takes you to the edge of the solar system. It doesn't take you into the galaxy that surrounds the solar system, as this density of communication doesn't extend that far. So chanting, and music, is very much about your emotional experience. It reflects very much what your state is at any given moment and how you experience it. The more complex the sound, the more you are experiencing and learning. The purer the sound (or that need for silence) and as you allow that higher portion of your being to establish itself more, the more you are released from the denser emotions of fear, anxiety and grief.

Have you noticed that when you mourn you often mourn on a particular note. The mourning is about letting go, but the mourning is also about acknowledging who you are, what you are, what you embrace as an individual and what you are not. The importance of mourning then, when it comes from the heart, also creates an effect that allows the spirit of the one who has departed to be raised into a higher vibratory state. The natural response, as odd as this may sound, of grief, of loss, or indeed of selfishness (as you feel sorry for yourself because you will not see, in your terms, the individual again) is actually an instinctive response acknowledging your being, and everybody else known to that individual, as they respond in their way too, creating a magnetic tunnel which supports the departed consciousness to attaining its height more comfortably, and with a greater sense of purpose. Not to mourn is to deny your life. To deny your life is to deny your perpetuation through time. It is non-being.

You have reached a time where non-being can no longer be possible. This is happening now. What is coming your way as you head into the new millennium is a greater resonance from this strata of the galaxy beyond your solar system, and this music of the spheres is being directed very much to those who want to avail themselves of it; is giving everyone their potential to step outside what you would call conditioned belief to conceive what is possible and to reject anything that is imposed that causes you to feel restricted. The collective force within the solar system is bringing about an instability, a dynamic instability that will, in time, make a quantum leap into a new state of being. The quantum leap at the level that we perceive it is way beyond your lifetimes, but nevertheless, the momentum is already reaching a critical point, where the instability is rooting out every other instability that surrounds it. You may experience this as chaos. You may experience this as political instability; people looking beyond religion for their own understanding. Looking beyond cultural support for ways in which to support their being. And this, in terms of your empathising being, creates stress, pain, anxiety. If you can allow yourselves to float above this, you will see quite clearly not only why this is being created but it will also allow you to recognise the effect that this is having and how certain people are responding. That is the most important thing: to be able to maintain the degree of peace as you move through the chaos.

Musically, it is time for the world to re-experience the pure note. So that you can experience the sacredness of your being that has been lost. As you examine the last approximately 150 years, technology has raced ahead at the expense of spirituality, which has left most people feeling sterile. The technological revolution brings with it its own new language, its own sounds. These sounds are based on or relative to machine or the inanimate as opposed to the animate, and there is a very strong need for you to recapture the animate – your own primeval cry – so that you can reverberate within that cry and recapture your harmonic which allows you to get a sense of direction. This direction may not be conscious, and it goes beyond the parameter of what you perceive as time but nevertheless it is present, it is already there. To meditate on sound, we are suggesting, is going to become more and more important. Not on the collectivity of sound but on the pure notes.

Are there any questions ?

*Could you explain the relationship between crystals, sound, light and colour please ?*

Every substance has sound contained within, latent or otherwise. Every substance has a particular vibration. If you look at the quality of the crystal which has very strong light qualities, within it there are a myriad of prisms that bend and reflect and absorb light in a very complex relationship. Understand also that the sound configurations contained within those crystals are also very complex, and the power of the crystal lies in the complexity of how it can communicate. The reason why they are greatly revered and appreciated is because of what they communicate. You may not always know why or what. You may feel their healing benefit. You may enjoy seeing them because of the colours they absorb and reflect. You may be able to activate their sound, which is not human but is nevertheless living and present. They have properties that relate to you, to plants, to everything within the physical earth plane in a way that no other composite material can. This would apply to all crystalline formation you have on earth. There are different crystals with different densities and different light forms which create different effects. You can imbue a crystal with a quality that will exude itself indefinitely. You can also change that quality. You can also activate within the crystal its own quality which can bring about harmony, disharmony, change, no change, as it sees fit. We won't say that it has a soul but it is very close to what we are, except we are not composed of matter. So the power is not understood by the human individual but the human individual does recognise the power. What you understand or know about the crystal is minute in comparison to its potential. You will come to realise the potential more and more.

*Can we recognise our own individual notes or find them in current music, or should we experiment with them ?*

It is better to experiment. The note, if you like, on the piano is a guideline but do understand that often your note will fall between the cracks as it may not exist, because when we talk about the sub-divisions within the notes and the sub-divisions within the sub-divisions, we are talking about fingerprinting within the note framework; yours will be unique. You will not hear it anywhere else. You can only hear it for yourself, with training. The more you familiarise yourself with sound, the closer you allow yourself to listen, for example, to one note, the easier it will be for you to hear your own.

*Is it important to recreate that note ?*

We have difficulty analysing that question because it demands an emotional response. It may be appropriate for us to say, that it can give you a greater sense of belonging.

*When listening to notes from another source, is it better to listen to the human voice, a note produced by an instrument or woodwind? Is there an order of preference ?*

Again we can't analyse this as it demands yet another emotional response. It is merely a reflection of your need. We would have to say, no, it doesn't matter.

*Would you clarify. We are made up of colour, light, sound and that sound has a certain trajectory through the solar system and out of the galaxy but on that trajectory there are spheres, we encounter certain spheres. What are those spheres?*

Consciousness forms that clarify experience. That is the simplest way we can define those.

*So, if I understand properly, does our trajectory – there is a buffer zone, you say that holes are appearing in that buffer zone to the galaxy outside our solar system – does our trajectory presently go through that? Have some people gone through that trajectory, through that buffer zone? Is that where we're aiming for?*

Yes to all of those.

*Can I go back to this pure note. Pure note was meant as an individual, a different note for each individual, not a collective note. Is there such a thing as a collective pure note, for let us say, humanity?*

Yes.

*Sorry, yes to what?*

Yes there is a collective note for humanity.

*But also a pure note for each individual ?*

Each individual has their own fingerprint in terms of their own experience of sound. That is unique to them. When we talk of the need, now, to listen to the pure note, we don't necessarily mean your own note. Very simply, one note on the piano, one string on the guitar, one string on the harp, whatever instrument, whatever sound. As you activate the sound of a crystal glass, that is sufficient. But just to experience, in your language, the sacredness of sound.

Bring your being inside yourself. Imagine a dome of light encompassing this group, coming to a point above the centre of the group that extends outward or upward. Get a sense of a crystal presence at that point. A note is being sounded at this point that represents the collective group note of all of you present. You may not hear, but listen and register what that means. Listen with your inner ear. Sometimes this sound is relative to your own and sometimes this sound is beyond it and sometimes you may hear this note through the noise of your own note. It is all dependent on your present condition. There is no need to feel that you have succeeded or failed at hearing this, the fact that you create alertness in the first instance is enough.

We begin to withdraw. Reflect on what has been said. Allow it to fill your being. Do not feel you have to make anything out of what has been said. It is merely what it is.

# FOUR

## *Action and Inaction*

As we equate our energy with, and draw our experience through, the human condition, it brings us to a point when it is important to look at the passive nature of the human being. To look at inertia. To look at dependency and expectation so that we have a whole perspective of the continuity through time, as the human perspective experiences it, and what that causes the human to carry with it in terms of tangible experience and understanding.

There has been, over the last millennium, an enormous passivity on earth, when humans have sat back, pursued the hedonistic nature of their material condition – not entirely to the exclusion of all else, but mostly to the exclusion of all else – bringing them to a point where they only perceive things in terms of the material, when it is very difficult for them to perceive things other than that which is material. This is particularly reflected within Western civilisation as you understand it now, presenting it with enormous problems in understanding what is beyond the material, namely the spiritual, the metaphysical. Looking beyond your galaxy, entertaining the possibility of what is beyond the galaxy and what that means in terms of impact of knowledge. Impact of knowledge. Knowledge itself is material because it is acquired and it is established. Consciousness. Stored information. The software in your hardware. But within the software, the thought, the information, the concepts are defined. And one of the greatest problems you have within society is not being open to what is possible. You define your reality very much only by what is, which in many ways causes you to have closed minds as you go about your daily life. Certainly, in terms of science, and the field of enquiry that science feels it has to assume, this is very obvious indeed. Scientists who move beyond what is defined are often perceived as irrational, betraying their integrity, by presenting non-facts to a world where everything is defined by those facts that you already have access to, not fully appreciating the philosophical need for the concept, understanding that the concept can often evoke in the individual something quite substantive.

The passivity is very much an emotional condition, and we include thought in this emotional condition. Your vessel often talks about thought as emotion. The moment that you create thought you develop an emotional relationship with it which causes you to define once again your reality. And whatever thought you define becomes belief which is in itself limiting by its very nature and existence. This emotional passivity, particularly now, evokes greed, the need to retain, and the need to empathise. You feel you're losing out if you don't join in on an experience, and if you don't join in on an experience, it means that you don't understand the person or the situation as well as you might, so you're losing out. You are failing to grasp what you need for knowledge. But this knowledge is really about survival. What we are trying to say in a convoluted way – it is convoluted because we don't emotionally relate to it – the issue is purely about survival. The will to live and motivation for life. How do you define life? How do you define the will to live? What does that mean to you? Does that purely mean sustaining yourself materially, not only in terms of money but in terms of what you eat and what you drink? Or is it also about allowing yourself to go beyond the premise of physical being? Now survival does not allow you to do that. It does not allow you to entertain possibility, so if you feel your life is truly about survival, you are in a very bad state indeed, because it means you are purely relating to your reality as you see it, not as you intuitively understand it, and certainly not in terms of concepts and intelligence; being able to look at situations as they are, not what you have to make them to be.

Survival, by the very definition of the word, is having a bad time, and all of you, as you debate whether your life is about survival or not, mean: Do you need to have a bad time or not? Do you have to join in with this very narrow perception of life? Are you going to allow life to be a passive experience? Are you going to allow yourself to be subject to what it has to offer to you? Or are you going to allow yourself to define, notice the world, live your life as you feel it needs to be. But defining your life as it needs to be may perhaps bring you to a point when there is no definition, which allows you to let go of any need to depend on or rely, or indeed, to expect. Very crudely, your life is creating an action to expect a reaction. Science teaches you that for every action there is an equal opposite reaction. That is a fundamental principal. But what if that reaction does not happen in your lifetime? What if the action that you create is beyond the material or beyond the physical? And how can you know when that reaction will happen? Do we all create actions whose impact can never be felt until we move into a different place? You would interpret this place as time. If we are talking about moving into a different place, we can be talking about thousands of years. When we are talking of anti-matter, the question is, can we create an action in anti-matter where that will only create another action, not another reaction? That, in many ways, goes against the nature of science itself. So be it. But the premise which this is based on merely defines physical experience. But we must never forget we can move beyond that, and indeed that we do exist beyond that physical premise. Understand that there are reactions that go far beyond time and place, which you create, but will never experience within the physical condition of life. So to define yourself is really not to give yourself the room to see what is possible or to be able to entertain the orchestrated movement, the harmonies and the levels of experience which we know permeate all time and space.

As your earth reality is experiencing this enormous passivity, we will go back to scientific definition. There has to be a reaction within your physical sense of the word to this specificity. In non-action there has to be a reaction of this non-action. Let us draw a mental picture. If this passivity, or non-action, is a vortex or a vacuum, that draws energy in on itself like an implosion, there has to be an echo of this in a non-physical way within the galaxy as you see it. And this other vortex of experience will create non-action within its space and time, but as this extends into the galaxy and beyond the galaxy, this non-action, very simply, creates a stillness. And this stillness, by the properties of magnetic attraction, is drawn into your reality – this is very difficult for us to describe – but draws into your reality an atmosphere that, very simply, creates change. We perceive this like cartilage between the bones, between the earth and what is beyond the earth, and within this place there is a dynamic instability which is quite still, focused and very direct. But this instability, by its very nature, will remove all other instability relative to itself, which as far as you're concerned, is to do with passivity. And it will make a leap, when it can no longer contain itself, into a new state of being. Again the principal is scientific in terms of your material reality. But what is this quantum leap from passivity into activity? It is already happening, but in a very minor way. There are very small ripples which we perceive as a dance of the vortices around the earth, and we see these very tiny pinpricks of light entering into your earth's environment, as people, individuals, pick up on this instability which gives them a sense of 'get up and go', which motivates them very directly in a particular way to understand what they are, not who they are, but what they are, which goes to the essence of their being. It is this which is creating an awareness of the spiritual dimension, of the metaphysical dimension and indeed, of the cosmic potential.

So to come back to the principle of passivity. It will reach a point where it won't contain itself any more, and individuals will begin to realise the need to understand self. Or they will create immense disharmony around themselves which may extend to groups, to communities, indeed it is possible, within whole civilisations, and there is also a possibility that these seven civilisations may actually experience a total breakdown. What that creates is a sense of individuality, not chaos or anarchy as it is politically defined, but a sense of individuality, of free-thinking nature. But again those free-thinkers establish a rapport with every other free-thinker, so that there is a new community within the cultural strata in which this occurs. Everybody begins to wake up, or at least, those that do band together in such a way that there is a sense of mutual support and harmony, and this is a direct reaction to passivity, and the passivity is merely trying to perpetuate what already exists. To continue to make comfortable what is already comfortable. But if that comfortableness is not progressive, if there is no sense of evolution or development, then there is simply that energy, which will break up and begin to dissipate because it has no real impact. You will notice this particularly within the great organisations, within politics, within religion; that they are no longer able to sustain themselves because the very fundamentals on which they are based, no longer have relevance or meaning. Again, you yourselves feel this very much emotionally. You feel this very much in terms of what you think and what you believe. And the more that you hang on to what is already established in your life, the more difficult it becomes to entertain any sort of possibility for change whatsoever. Do you really believe that you are so uncreative and unresourceful that you can't adapt, that you can't respond to change as change asserts itself? Do you really fundamentally believe that? Because if you do, your life is about survival and you have a problem. If you don't, your life is not about survival and it means you can use your intelligence to entertain what is possible. You want to know your purpose. Your purpose is to experience life. That is all. Spiritual development, as you define it, is creating an awareness of the metaphysical, that which is beyond physical. So that you can have a sense of this and get on with being human on a daily basis. So that you are aware of magnitude, of space, of time, which eases the pressure which allows you to take things less seriously. Each decision, although it has its value, may then become less important, because it may affect the grand order of events or maybe not, or maybe not in a way that you anticipate.

Passivity brings about clarity, vision, and total objectivity. That is the reaction. And you must understand that those people who are very much part of that reality are teaching the whole society, within which you live, a very precise lesson, if only you can allow yourself to see it in those terms. That lesson, fundamentally, is that there is another way of going about things, and that other way is not about denial, it is not about sacrifice. Denial and sacrifice are very much what you are taught to believe in. And denial and sacrifice very much create dependency and expectation. If I suffer, I will become a better person. If I sacrifice my need for someone else's need, it shows that I am compassionate. It shows that I am loving. It shows that I am responsible.

Does this really do something for yourself? Do you honestly allow yourself to entertain the possibility? Fundamentally, what do you have to prove? We don't expect an answer, but ask yourselves the question. When you leave this room tonight, ask yourselves, what do you have to prove? Is there anything? Is there anything at all? Or are you meant to use this life purely as a means to be intelligent? To be able to balance both sides of the argument without having to take sides, just being able to appreciate? To create goals – worthy as they are – often defines your life in a particular way, that causes you to ignore the experience of attaining goals. The experience is everything, as it broadens knowledge. Experience takes you beyond learning. Listen to the words. Experience breaks down knowledge and belief. You read, therefore you know. That is wrong. Experience, and in this way you shall understand. That is right. The understanding is part of your innate wisdom, and you can only understand by experiencing. You can understand the question. You can understand and experience the question, and having experienced a question often means that the answer is totally redundant. If you understand what you need, not what you desire, if you understand what you need in life, does that really mean that you have to attain it? Merely understanding what it represents is enough because it actually allows you to play. To become less serious. To be less involved. It allows you to observe, which is very important. How much do you see? How much are you alert to? How often have you stood on the street and watched people? Watch where people are coming from. Watch where they are walking towards, and how they do that. Do they do it with a sense of purpose? Are they lost in thought? Are they alert to other people around them? Do they give way to other people? Are they sensitive to other people's space? What does that say about that individual that you see walk down the street? Do you observe yourself? Do you actually sit and take stock? Do you actually watch what you do? Do you allow yourself to understand the patterns of behaviour you have in your life? It's not a question of whether you accept or not. But do you allow yourself to acknowledge them? For the more truthful a relationship you have with yourself, the more open you can be in terms of life. It creates less pressure. It means you're not dependent on other people to tell you what you are. It means that you don't expect people to behave in a particular way towards you. You do what you do because you need to. And that is all. There is no need for feedback. It is desirable, but it isn't needed. The desire fulfils the ego which allows the personality and the character to feel good. But that is such a superficial quality. What do you need to feel good? Is it so important? Can you allow the inner feeling, the inner sense of trust and awareness, can you allow that to give you a sense of what you are? So the feeling good becomes security of being, becomes peace, becomes tranquillity, becomes bliss and the experience of bliss; that joy of wisdom connecting with unconditional love that permeates the universe and time and space. That bliss goes beyond all trauma, all fear, all restriction. You have chaos all around you. The chaos will never stop. Does this mean you give up and do nothing? If it doesn't, then what do you do? Do you set about righting the world? Or do you set about understanding the world and the state that it's in and why it is in that state? You cannot right experience. You are not spilling a glass of water. Once you have spilt the glass of water, it is very difficult to put all that water back in the glass. To be able to equate that with experience, which has no real substance at all, is virtually incomprehensible. So do not try to right the experience. The experience is allowed to be exactly what it is. Past. History. But what you can do is create a new experience which may create an environmental happening that is totally different from the previous experience. The more you understand life as being about possibility, and continuity within possibility, you have exactly what life is about.

As we communicate with you now we are aware of your possibility, we are also aware of our possibility. But our possibility as you are witnessing and hearing and experiencing now in this room, is very different from how it is for us, as we have no form, shape or definition. We are merely an accumulation of different essences and it is only the essences that can experience, purely for themselves. We see you as one, yet you are many. We see you as a state of being, and yet we do appreciate the individuality within the state of being. You yourself, as we have explained before, are an accumulation of dense, physical memory. Very highly specialised memory. But the density of it creates a problem. But that problem creates motivation or the impulse to do, and it is that impulse which we see as life, and that life has to be experienced. Dependency within love, for the human condition, is a very large issue. Love, emotional love, romantic love, is really projecting your needs on to another human being in the hope or anticipation that they can receive and respond to them in a compatible way. And you rely on each other to do this. If one doesn't cooperate, there is a breakdown in this scenario. Now if we look at the evolution of romantic love, there are certain qualities that we bring into the situation of companionship, partnership, marriage, being together with another human individual. We bring into this detachment freedom, both physical freedom, professional freedom, mental freedom, and indeed the freedom to love. And we require, or you require, that other individual to acknowledge that. This is nothing to do with physical promiscuity. This is nothing to do with being disloyal, in terms of heartfelt feelings to another human being, but what it does mean is that there is a certain universality about this experience which allows you to be, or to live, with one individual without limiting your experience of others around you. And we do mean that in terms of romantic love. What you have within your civilisation at the moment is great difficulty in maintaining any situation which involves dependency; dependency as it relates to the emotional condition, and this doesn't necessarily have to be confined to romantic love. What people intuitively are beginning to understand for themselves is: How can I project what I need when I don't understand need? And how can I possibly have what I need reciprocated when that fundamental understanding hasn't already been established? So the revolution that is already present within society is making people aware of their fundamental needs. This, at a very basic level, is what you perceive as New Age. The term is not a good one and the term can only ultimately bring about a sense of limitation, because it defines and seems to bring about a definition, by virtue of its seemingly unlimiting context. But all seemingly unlimiting contexts themselves begin to introduce within themselves certain parameters and belief structures to which you need to adhere, to be part of that Age.

Within the next few hundred years, then, we have a totally different emotional state of being. This does not mean that individuals may not encounter this long before then. Indeed there are many within the earth at the moment who not only have experienced this but are already going beyond that into what comes after. Expectation is the human thinking, 'If I do this I will get something in return because I deserve it'. And when that doesn't happen, the human being either stops and does something else, or becomes more obsessive with that original function until he or she believes they get their just deserts. Expectation creates a certain hiatus around the whole environment of the earth itself. This hiatus has a certain attraction, and it draws towards it – it is again very difficult for us to describe – a dissolving quality, and this dissolving quality doesn't take away expectation, it doesn't dissolve the expectation, it actually increases the expectation to such a degree that it can no longer contain itself any more and then breaks up, as a magnifying glass under the sun can actually create fire and this hiatus is very effective in destroying. It breaks down. Be aware of this in your own life and, as you observe your own expectations, witness whether they are fulfilled or not, and if they're not fulfilled, how you react. Do you leave it be and move onto something else, or do you become more obsessive? If you become more obsessive, ultimately what happens? Within our own reality, we don't have obsession as you understand it. But we have a certain inward focus, like boring a black hole in space and that black hole permeates all space where there is non-action. You would say where there is no experience, where it seems nothing happens, where there is no feedback, ultimately there is no stimulation. But this inward vision allows us to understand the nature of non-matter and it allows us to build structure within non-matter that can protect energy as it exists. This non-matter can enclose consciousness and physical space and isolate it. It is perfectly feasible for us to create non-matter, for example, around a star, so that it is not visible to you on Earth and to remove all effects, energetically, that the star has on the environment around it, from happening. For us, what you would call obsession, can be a very productive and constructive situation. It can be a very deliberate way to build rather than deconstruct – to take out of service might be a phrase you could identify with as being associated with this process – as it isn't required, or the intensity is too much at a particular point.

Your feelings and emotions lack definition, which is why you have difficulty with them. Despite what we said, that most actions, thoughts, beliefs and sensations within your world are quite defined and dense, by their very nature, the origin of feelings which very much relate to your intuitive being is not defined. Which is why you can never make them into anything. Which is why they are so elusive. The human has great difficulty in understanding that feelings are a reaction or by-product of experience. That is all. And this by-product is there merely to allow you to understand. You don't put them in a box. You don't try to shape them in any way. There is no coherent manner in which these feeling should behave. As a result of this, there is no way in which you can clearly observe how these feelings work. The response is important and to acknowledge the response is also important, which means you are being open and truthful. Then you let these feelings and sensations be. They tell you what's happening. Within love, the need to perpetuate or the desire to perpetuate a sense of continuity within these feelings again often brings about problems as you try to define them, and give them focus in a way they don't need.

Love is about freedom in its unconditional sense. If you try to define that love, it brings you to a point of passivity. A sense of inertia that comes from this passivity. We will have to build a mental picture as it is hard for us to describe. For the inertia that is created almost becomes a weight that sinks into the earth, and that weight, which is purely energy or consciousness, brings about physical change within the earth's structure. This is immensely difficult for us to describe. That there is a reciprocal relationship to you and the earth. Understand that whatever you create, everything within your solar system has to react as a result. You notice this mostly in terms of your earth, for example, the atmosphere, how the pressure within the atmosphere is changing. How there is a very slight alteration within the gravitational force and how gravity works. The ionic sphere which is around the earth itself. How this is adapting, how this is changing. The sense of accumulation of moisture that is taking place within this ionosphere, how that is creating in many ways a greater density within the earth which ultimately is going to bring about change, a molecular change, within the lungs, within the respiratory system, and within the blood. Physiologically, this is where you notice the greatest change, within the blood, the lungs, the heart and the circulatory system. You will notice this with disease. Disease is often perceived in your reality as the precursor to change. The first thing that makes you aware that something is happening. Illness is very much a breakdown of society. Not of anything moral or anything to do with belief, but a breakdown in physiology that makes you aware of how physiological change is going to come about. If you look at many of the contemporary diseases that relate strongly to the nature of the blood and the lungs, and the accumulative effectiveness that these diseases are having within the earth, you are alerted to how you could stop the diseases happening. You can't, but what you are alerted to is some of the complementary causes, the accumulation of causes, that contribute to these particular diseases. These then alert you to certain social conditions, to certain atmospheric conditions, which brings about a whole field of enquiry relating to certain aspects of illness, which focuses your attention on physical change within the earth, be it atmospheric, be it constitutional, by which we mean relating to what you eat and what you drink. Again, part of the inertia and the passivity that exists on the earth gives way to these diseases very fruitfully in a very real way. But do understand that you learn from these diseases; your awareness is heightened and those individuals who encounter these diseases encounter them for a very specific reason, and they are acting with real spiritual courage and determination.

The collective way in which the consciousness and unconsciousness work and relate to each other, is very intimate and very progressive. We do appreciate that it is often very difficult for you to see and understand this, at the level it is happening. But everything within your society, the way that communication is received, digested and absorbed, means that the privileged few are becoming more aware, and the privileged few, look not only at the cause but the effect, not only in the world but the possible effect in terms of universal understanding. You can only do what you can do. Your own individual development as a human being means that you are more alert. That is all you need to do. Be more alert. Literally, see better, sense and trust that sense, because that sense is individual to you and works for you. It doesn't work for anyone else. Your vessel often talks about the decline of mediumship, as it is understood, and from our perception this is absolutely right, for, as individuals' ability to do it for themselves is increasing, the medium becomes redundant. That does not mean to say that there won't be seers, that the psychic reality itself becomes redundant. That is not what we mean. We are talking about communication between different realities. Being able to justify and clarify to people something which is beyond their perception to do. There is a general increase in sensitivity. We mean this psychically within each individual in the earth plane. This sensitivity, again, is a direct effect from passivity, alerting you more to your creative nature and how that can be expressed. That is all.

You feel you need to achieve. You feel you need to have goals, to aim for things. That isn't what life is about. Relax more, with your own sense of enjoyment. Allow yourself to experience as much as you possibly can, and don't apologise for that experience. As a race you are very judgemental and when you begin to sense this judgemental way in which you evaluate your reality, it often means that you lose your sense of justice. We don't mean the difference between that which is right and that which is wrong. It is more to do with appropriateness. Ultimately, there is no compromise. Ultimately, there is no giving-in to others. But ultimately, what we do have is a dovetailing, as each individual can understand other people's needs. That is all. That is all that concerns the evolution of life in all spheres, in all dimensions, in all realities. Which is why there is no stillness as each dovetailing experience ricochets through all time and space, and as it is completed in one place, that initiates its taking place in another place.

The greatest conflict around your globe is based only on greed and the inability to move forward. It is really only based in lack of generosity and compassion, which is why there are many healers recognising their own power. This is not to say that each one of these individual healers needs to heal, it is merely to do with the evocation of compassion. So the spiritual revolution is about allowing everybody to understand the true nature of compassion, which is spiritual and cosmic in its own nature of origin. It is your job merely to make people aware of this compassion. You are fundamentally love, and when your physical body is no longer required, it is to love that you return. And when your spiritual body is not longer required, you become closer to this essence of love as it truly is, as you will no longer need to experience emotional love, romantic love, as you have it presently.

The explanations may seem lengthy and convoluted. We don't mean them to be. We are merely trying to create a greater perspective and picture of your reality, just to allow you to feel your space. Your room. To allow you to give yourself permission to be flexible and adaptable so that you can have your own love and your own truth.

Are there any questions ?

*What is your understanding of God?*

A unifying force of love that creates a cosmic stickiness that creates the impulse for integration.

*Can that be thought of as personality or is it best thought of as a love or a force or an energy?*

It is more the latter. The sense, the energy quality, the consciousness that infinity of being represents, not personality. It cannot be, as God represents something different for each reality. You perceive it as a personality because you are personality. We are hardly matter. We perceive it as hardly matter. Those other realities that are beyond matter perceive it in their own light. In many ways God, for you, is part of the projection, it is part of the need to identify, in an emotional way, and you feel you can only give yourself away to a personality. You feel you can't always give yourself away to an essence because what does that mean? But essence is the closest to what we perceive.

*To what extent are we capable of changing our reality through meditation and visualisation ?*

You don't change your reality, you change your ability to perceive your reality, which frees you creatively as an individual, which makes you more capable of doing more. The meditative device is merely creating space in the mind. The space in the mind is nothing, and in nothing there is everything, all possibility, and the more that you allow your mind to experience all possibility, the greater the flexibility, the more creative you feel you are.

We will bring this evening to a close. Reflect on the questions that have been asked. Hold them in your heart. Allow them to be special to you because you are important.

# FIVE

# Experience of Psychic Space

To allow us to facilitate understanding further we need to explain and elaborate on psychic space. There are many ways in which the word psychic is defined or interpreted. We would like you to bear in mind the definition 'that which leads to the essence' as being the closest. The word psychic and space indicate two specific areas: space, in terms of dimension, and space in terms of what is contained within one particular place, so that when we look at psychic space, we look at being able to perceive essence within different dimensions of truth and also being able to look at the essence within a particular position. Again we have to come back to time and we have to ask you to remember that time is closer to position than duration, so that even when we talk about position or place, for you this often involves or embraces time as well, though we may not talk of time. For us time has little to do with duration. We cannot equate what we say very well with duration though that is how you measure your own life and experiences. When we look at dimension, you have the physical, the spiritual, the cosmic. You have matter, you have non-matter which as we have explained before is very different from matter, and is also different from anti-matter. Matter: dense substance, dense experience, dense feeling. Non-matter: feeling which is not dense, sensations which have no context and experience which hasn't yet been known. Anti-matter: that which goes beyond the law of science as you understand it. Within those three parameters there are distinct realities that operate with their own parameters, so that as you approach each of these dimensions they have very specific laws that operate in very specific ways, and you can be sure that as you enter each of these realities, they have something to offer that is unique to themselves.

We talked previously about experiencing what your vessel calls 'living beyond the box'. You know what living in the box is. You can sense everything, you can see everything, you can hear everything within the box. Outside the box, you don't know whether anything exists, and if anything does you certainly haven't experienced it before. When you do experience something outside the box, there is nothing to relate it to. That doesn't mean to say that nothing exists here, nor does it mean that what you have experienced doesn't exist. You can apply this in terms of your own emotional being as well as non-material being. In many ways what you haven't experienced relates directly to non-material being, even if that experience is contained within your emotional reality, but again, that is another dimension within your physical existence. The altered state of reality allows you to experience more. For example, when you meditate you enter into an altered state of being. This altered state of being is given many sorts of definitions within your reality, anything from the lower astral to the spiritual which allows you to perceive your own emotional material reality with greater clarity. In effect, what you are doing is moving through the higher vibrational frequency of the whole of your emotional being that allows you to experience what you need to before it actually happens, giving you a sense of preparation or precognition. That alerts you to what is possible, alerts you to the experience and allows you to be better prepared. Your dream state allows you the opportunity to experience what you don't have time for during your normal day. It also allows you to resolve situations that you don't need to experience within the conscious working part of your day as well. It also, naturally, gives you that sense of freedom to move in the upper vibrational state of your being, albeit unconsciously, to experience the different aspects of yourself as they exist within a particular place. This place may embrace more than just a physical reality. It may also embrace your spiritual being, and it may embrace the cosmic or blueprint. So that not only are you experiencing extending that experience, resolving and also preparing your being for the impact of new experience, you are also assimilating information at a very rapid rate. By virtue of your physical presence on earth, no matter where you allow yourself to drift or explore in terms of consciousness, everything registers within your genetic being. Everything is transmitted. So even though you may not be consciously aware of that, nevertheless, you do know that it becomes present within your being. To be able to reflect on what you have dreamt can be important, but do realise that often the dreams will remain incoherent as the experiences are so multi-dimensional, involving so many different aspects of your being, that it is very difficult for your conscious mind to hold all of that in one instance. So to actually assimilate and digest that information becomes virtually impossible. The dreams, therefore, become, in your words, surreal, and because there doesn't seem to be a context, it is difficult for you to translate this information into practical knowledge.

When you are asleep, imagine yourselves as hedgehogs and that around you you have a band of energy which has many funnels of energy emanating from your body into free space. Each of these funnels gives you access to the various realities which you naturally have contact with, and your astral body can be led, or magnetised, through any one of these tunnels in order to gain experience, and from this experience a registration takes place that allows your psyche to acknowledge what has taken place. Again, this doesn't have to be conscious, but nevertheless, it is imprinted in your being, what has been experienced and what that means to you. To give you an example, we will relate this to what your vessel is experiencing at the moment.

His dream state is very restless and he rarely wakes refreshed, as the experience of his multi-dimensional being is so active. This is in direct relationship to the psychic quality that he holds within his being that allows him to explore. Within the context of this place, or in your words, time, there is an accelerated learning process in terms of his emotional being. As he is committed to living within the emotional context and continuing to experience within the emotional context, this causes him to have to experience a reality which he has chosen, although it is not necessary for him, and so, as there is no need for it to be conscious, it is done within the dream state and this emotional extension brings him into many different complex relationships with his family, allowing him to relate, not only to his own family, but to all mothers, fathers and brothers within family situations through time. So whatever frustrations there have been in the past, whatever frustrations are likely to be there in the future, are defined by karma, and are being brought to a close. Where this might have happened in a future time, what he has effectively chosen is to diminish, or indeed remove, certain of these experiences entirely from future karmic presence here on earth, to bring all of this emotional friction to a close. By choosing to experience emotionally he is removing his need for physical presence on the earth in future time. However, we have to say, because this time is relative to this place that he already occupies, this future time is meaningless. So the accelerated learning process relates very precisely to place but as we try to put this in context with time, it has little value. It is all part of the same experience. It also – as he resolves his emotional karma, and, metaphorically speaking, energy leaves his being – creates a vacuum that draws in a further energy or consciousness that fills the gap. This other energy consciousness has no substance. This other energy consciousness is non-matter. It has being within it but this being is beyond his experience and this being creates very small energy bridges between the cells and, as the cells are separating, these little bridges create in many ways new cells, but these new cells have no substance. They are non-matter. But, because of their progressive experience within one place or time, they already have a memory even though there is no substance. As that memory is being transmitted to the DNA itself, the DNA is already in a state of preparation for non-matter. We hope that you are following. As, therefore, we are looking at the human body in evolutionary terms reaching a point when matter is no longer sustained and your energy body just glows, so you move from matter to non-matter, from substance to non-substance and the impact of all of this experience within your vessel's make up means that this transition is perfectly natural. These non-material cells are already building up in and around him. These bridges are holding together his emotional being as he continues to experience emotionally, but these bridges are maintaining more substance. His ability to draw cosmic information, to draw from the blueprint exactly 'what is' becomes increased so his potential to hold understanding, to hold the capability of understanding, becomes much greater which, in turn, allows him the opportunity to bring this understanding into conscious knowledge. We hope you are following what we are saying. It is rather difficult as we don't emotionally relate to what we are trying to explain. By using your vessel as an example, we wish you to relate to it as this is also happening to you. We have to talk in terms of place, not time, and within this place of experience, this is happening to you.

Earlier, we talked of this displacement of emotion and feeling that many people, many groups within society, are experiencing. We now wish to relate this to that we have just described. Although this may sound strange, the way that you feel, the way that you sense, the way that you intuit, is becoming different. Your need to relate is becoming different. How you relate and why is redefined. This has to be understood. This has not only to do with the change in psychology as you have to reorientate yourself with life and what life is or is not offering to you; it is to do with a state of being, and this must be fully appreciated. If it isn't fully appreciated, then the whole premise of presenting the explanation has no substance whatsoever.

When we move into non-material, non-emotion, non-feeling, non-experience, we talk of you being able to enter into spheres of knowledge which allow you to get a sense of the totality of the universe. These spheres of knowledge have a sense of containment about them. These spheres, literally, have energy-form, no substance, but energy-form, and as your consciousness draws to itself these spheres, it allows you both consciously and unconsciously to enter into them, to experience outside the box. Understand that the principle of the box is limiting, and that each box in turn can disappear as you experience more outside it, as what you experience outside the box becomes more important than what you have within and the box itself disappears. But then, because you are human and you have the need to believe, you create another box that contains what you then know. You have Russian dolls where you have a large doll and inside this doll you have a smaller doll, and inside this doll you have a smaller doll still. The principle is the same. There are no limits to the number of boxes that you can create within your physical condition, and you create them to feel secure, but that is only to maintain a superficial state of being. So non-matter represents what you can't possibly anticipate and what you can't possibly know. Please remember, this does not mean that you can't experience and that you can't know. This non-matter, although it embraces emotions is largely beyond emotional experience. As you have a suspension bridge, this non-matter is in the middle of the bridge between the spiritual and the cosmic. It is a neutral place which offers you the opportunity to experience, without influence, without dogma, without teaching, without reason and without the need to justify. More and more you will find that you have the ability to reach this neutral place. Many may say this is within the mind, or this is above the mind, or you do this through your higher self. The definition doesn't really matter. The fact that this place exists does matter, and your ability to reach and experience it is increasingly becoming much better. It is neutral because it is free from emotion, which is limiting; neutral because it isn't as threatening as the cosmic, which has no real way to relate to the personal emotional, so that you aren't taken to a place where you are unable to facilitate consciousness, absorb it, and digest it. It is there to provide an emotional release, to give you a sense of belonging and to allow you to feel at home. Some of you are already talking of moving beyond the spiritual which brings to light the question: Is there a place or is there an experience beyond the spiritual? Yes, indeed, there is, and in many ways it is what we are trying to explain. But you ask yourself the question: How do we know that there is something beyond the spiritual when we haven't experienced it before, and when the great teachers of the world or the great spiritual teachers haven't made us aware of this before? Again we say, if the great spiritual teachers have waited for you to arrive at the point when you're able to liberate yourselves sufficiently, to be able to explore this on your own without the need for guidance or spiritual teaching, then the spiritual teachers are indeed paying you the greatest compliment by acknowledging that you can do this on your own. Because there is a very great need for you to do it on your own. We have already explained that if there are teachers here on earth who, recently, have begun to be aware of the cosmic presence and what that means, and the information, the resolution, the context that this cosmic understanding can present each individual, then this transmission of information, for you, is new. This information alerts you to a new view, a new vista, a new reality.

See yourselves as a tube of toothpaste, and this tube of toothpaste belongs to a very large household, who have many friends who all come round to brush their teeth. The toothpaste container is your physical body, your emotional being, and it has to be flexible, it has to be able to mould itself to whatever pressure is brought to bear on it. The toothpaste itself is your own personal wisdom and understanding, and the toothpaste coming out of the tube is you bringing that forth to yourself, and eventually into the world itself. The people who squeeze the toothpaste relate to your spiritual consciousness and your cosmic consciousness, so the flexibility that you have to exercise yourselves, and indeed that you have to endure, is enormous. The feeling you have to endure is something that is becoming particularly strident at the moment, as you seek to have joy and peace in a place where joy and peace appear to be anathema. Again you have to understand that, in this place, a point has been reached where your reality, where consciousness within your reality is being raised to a higher vibratory level. This is going to create pressure, emotional pressure, psychological pressure, pressure on what you believe, and you feel this emotionally. You feel this pressure within the fluid which runs up and down the spine, and the spinal meninges and cerebral meninges themselves are becoming stretched in a way they have never experienced. Being able to rebalance the energy within the spine and within the head is now for you becoming very important. The movement of the bones within the skull is becoming more noticeable. The need for very subtle re-arrangement of the bones within the skull is becoming important, so that the pressure within the cranial cavity and within the spinal column can be adjusted. What you have as the vibration increases within these cavities, is the bone matter trying to adapt to this increase in vibration. The bone contains and holds the vibration and this resonates within the cavities. This creates stress, and it upsets the calcium and potassium balance within the body. We were talking before of how important it is to maintain this potassium and calcium balance, because fundamentally we are talking about maintaining the electronic charge within the cell. As the cells separate, as the bonding mechanism between the cells becomes more flexible, without the electronic charge within the cell being maintained, it means that the individual is likely to experience great distress within the spine and within the head. This mainly relates to the nervous system, but if there is any breakdown in communication within the nervous system as it spreads into the physical body, it can lead to distress within certain physical organs, or related to specific physiological function. There is no need to go into great depth about this, but there is a need to understand. Very simply – and we don't mean to alarm – we are merely saying it in this way because there is no other way for us to say it – is that the bones are becoming brittle. Women in particular, who experience enormous swings in terms of their hormonal make-up, are particularly susceptible to the change of the electronic charge within the cellular walls. Men experience this as well, but in many ways, it is women who are leading the field by experiencing it, and thus showing medicine what needs to be done. Women are the bearers of life. Karmically, they have taken it upon themselves to demonstrate how to grow and evolve. That is how it is. Men cooperate and help to facilitate this. Their function in many ways is to serve and understand the bringers of life. That is a very simple karmic illustration, and you mustn't forget that as you move through time you experience being both woman and man. We use this illustration only to facilitate a greater understanding, not that it should lead to political debate.

As we move into anti-matter, do please appreciate that it is very difficult for us to explain something that is beyond emotional experience and that there is no way in which you can fully understand what this state means. We appreciate both our difficulty in explaining and your difficulty in receiving information, which allows us or causes us to be rather reticent about explaining further what is contained within the anti-matter state. All we wish to say is that often matter reaches its point of relative stillness where there is very little that it needs to experience to gain further understanding, and when that happens it evolves almost into a mirror image of itself that is inversely proportional to its matter state, which gives it a sense of experience of progression in a way that we cannot describe. However, what we would like to say is that the more you evolve and grow, the more you are able to entertain of the idea of the cosmic within the neutral place which we have already illustrated exists, then the more your potential to experience anti-matter becomes real. We cannot relate to this in terms of time, but when you reach that point of experience, that is when the coordinates of where you currently now live and experience direct you into a totally different place altogether. Some of you experience anti-matter. Some of you already have a sense of what that may mean. That is all. You don't need to know any more, you don't need to explain or justify it in any way. To do that would be inadequate and unfulfilling. It is sufficient for you to realise that you have now reached an evolutionary point when your ability to move into non-matter is becoming very real, and also vital. This is a place of experience where you can go to get a sense of self. To get a sense of self that is beyond problems, that is beyond friction. That gives you a sense of being beyond self. Your vessel talks about spiritual development and personal development as giving every individual a greater sense of self. So to experience beyond self gives you a sense of belonging to a greater whole. As you may find yourselves becoming more detached, as you find yourself more and more clinically looking at situations and feeling that you are not involved any more, or that you don't have any empathic feeling towards certain situations any more, you actually do it from a point of confidence and that confidence allows you to know deep within yourself that you're not being cold and heartless, that you're not being dispassionate, but you are very sure of what you are, and what that means to yourself. Having reached that point, you can then look at self beyond self. Again, we hope you are following what we are trying to explain because the self beyond self actually allows you to understand what you are growing into, what you are becoming. This self beyond self, although it relates to emotions and feelings, doesn't have contained within it emotion and feeling, and this neutral place is not spiritual. Again it has no mass, it has no substance, but it does have form. It does have containment. That containment means that within it there is consciousness. When we talked about these spheres of light, and the harmonic orchestration that these spheres of light create when they are attracted to your harmonic, this in many ways is what we mean. Because these spheres of light are allowing you to have a sense of your own personal worth and direction.

# SIX

# The Earth as Memory

We wish to map out for you this evening the different frequencies that enter the earth environment and how these frequencies relate to specific life-forms, to examine their complementary relationship and to give you an emotional sense of what these different vibrations represent. We will look primarily at the three Kingdoms you have on earth: the Animal, the Plant and the Human Kingdoms. It is necessary to remove the Human from the Animal as the frequencies on which you both exist are radically different.

Imagine a net coming together at a physical point in space and from this net extend many different fibres, and these matrices embrace everything within it. On Day 1, whenever that was, this net extended several of its branches into the earth to support a different cellular type memory, to give it a sense of existence and belonging; also to give these cellular existences a sense of connection with what is beyond the earth, so that they can have some sense of continuity, and place, within time and space. In the beginning, the net was wide. It was variegated and it extended into many different crude life forms. As these life forms matured and evolved, some of these vibratory frequencies blended with each other to become a more complex whole of a particular aspect, bringing you to the point where you now have your three Kingdoms as we define them. There is a point of definition where each becomes one and the same thing, or one and the same aspect, but presently in your current position they are defined in three particular ways. When we look at the Plant Kingdom, we are looking at a complementary energy-force that generally helps to sustain a life-force or an energy that helps create an environment within the framework of not only the earth but the solar system, that sustains a very particular life-force. Consequently, the indigenous memory peculiar to the complex genetic make-up of all flora within the earth relates very much to itself, no matter how complex, no matter how different each plant or each algae is to the other. The cellular memory, as it comes to its own point within the context of the Plant Kingdom, allows it to understand the complementary nature of its being. So the earth, as a receptor of information, as a database which holds and releases this information into the Plant Kingdom, acts as a filter for what it receives from within the physical universe. The earth acts thus as a filter mechanism, for memory, for different impulses, and for different progressions that it needs to hold within it, so that information can actually be transmitted to what the earth holds on its surface and within itself. Thus the earth is very much a living organism. But it has the ability – almost as your brain feeds mechanical movement and mechanical operation – to do this in terms of the Animal, Human and the Plant Kingdoms. So the information that it actually feeds to the Plant Kingdom is collective rather than selective. And each plant has the ability, not only to refine for itself exactly what it needs, but to sense genetically how every other form of plant-life is evolving. Each plant or species then naturally understands, not only what is required of it, but also how other plant life is evolving. It is able to judge then, how much it needs to reproduce, how much it needs to spread over the face of the earth so that life force can be maintained. This information is very much contained at a cellular level, but as far as science is concerned, it can't be measured or examined within the DNA structure within the plant cell itself. This memory is contained within water. As within homeopathic philosophy, there is the ability to transmit memory through water to bring a very fine essence of a particular treatment to an aqueous solution. Understand that in vibrational terms, the earth can communicate what is required into any form of aqueous solution. Consequently, any plant form that draws on water for nourishment, immediately has access to that information and immediately can refine that information for itself. Understand also that as the earth respires and gives moisture into the atmosphere, there is other plant life which doesn't draw nourishment or water directly from the earth but from its surrounding environment. Consequently, what is contained within the moisture also has within it certain vibratory forces which act as a conduit or a transmitter, conveying this information to the plant-form that absorbs moisture in this way. The particular vibratory forces that work collectively with the flora have a very specific function. The best way that we can explain this is to maintain a consistency in fluidity, so that the specific gravity within which the earth is contained remains progressively constant. This does not mean to say that it remains the same, but we say it is progressively constant because as it evolves it needs to be balanced within its evolution.

When we look at the Animal Kingdom, we are looking at a very different frequency that actually supports the fauna on earth, so that there is a continuity of information. Again, we look at the vibrational nature of particular life forms within the Animal Kingdom. You have to look at what the animal eats and what the animal drinks, and in what part of the world the animal sustains itself. Within the Animal Kingdom you have those who are entirely vegetarian and those that exist on other animals for their own nourishment, so that within the Animal Kingdom there are two ways information is absorbed. One from the natural frequency that comes from the earth through the cellular memory of plants which is then absorbed into the animal, so that continuity of memory or remembering is maintained. And the second, that within the Animal Kingdom who feed off other animals, off flesh. Flesh, being more dense, has a different frequency to it, a different sort of memory. The animal that feeds of flesh competes more, is more aware of its need to be in a place, a place where there is dense vibration.

Now do not take what we are about to say too seriously, we use the words merely to illustrate. When there are groups of people, or groups of animals, together in high concentration, in vibrational terms, these areas are dense. So that animals who need meat for sustenance will always naturally be drawn to higher concentrations of density, be they animal or human, it doesn't matter. The vibration is very similar, even though we make a distinction between both of these Kingdoms. But the density means that they respond very closely to the human, and that the human observes their behaviour more easily in terms of themselves rather than being rather bemused by the animal who feeds merely off plant life. It is very difficult for us to talk of behaviour because it is only an outward manifestation of consciousness. It does not actually explain the consciousness, in this case of the animal itself. When we enter into the consciousness of both these divides within the Animal Kingdom, and when we look at the vegetarian, we are looking at the animal who is more alert to vibrational change. We are looking at the animal who is more alert to atmospheric change and their immediate instinct is to follow this atmospheric change. With regard to the animal who feeds on flesh, they are less alert to these stimuli and it means they can remain in dense situations for longer periods than the vegetarian can because its ability to survive is more crude. Its ability to gain sustenance in harsher realities is much greater. We cannot really say that the vegetarian animal is more sensitive than the meat eating animal but there is a certain frequency here that, in terms of its consciousness and in terms of its own understanding, requires the vegetarian to be more mobile than the meat eating animal. It also means that the environment that can sustain the vegetarian is also more fragile and even though the vegetarian animal may be more flexible and adaptable, it is actually more threatened by environmental change than the denser meat-eating animal. Putting these two together to use as a form and indeed a very crude form of comparison, what they – again in a very crude way – reflect to the Human Kingdom, is very reasonable indication of environmental change and what that means in terms of whole earth consciousness. On the one hand you have the vegetarian animal being very subtly influenced and alert to universal cellular memory, and on the other, we have the meat-eating animal who is very alert to change within density; so that it is, in a very crude way, aware of change within society, not only of its own society but any society that has a density about it. Again we remind you of the density of the Human Kingdom.

So, depending on the occurrence of particular species on the earth, depending on their location and depending on their change of habit, the Human Kingdom can understand how invasive or to what degree it invades the natural reality of the flora and fauna on earth. So as we look at the particular frequencies that influence the Animal and the Plant Kingdom, we see that they act as a template or a blueprint which allows the human to understand its own historical evolution and allows it to gain some insight into what it is destroying and the effect that that will have on the Human Kingdom in general. It is easier to understand the Human Kingdom for you are human. But as you understand that you are predominantly water and as we have suggested that you are, as individuals, going to become less dense, then your ability to draw in to your aqueous state the more subtle vibrations that the Plant Kingdom is already able to assimilate becomes much greater. It allows every human individual the opportunity to be able to sense, not necessarily know, but to sense what is happening within the earth plane; what is happening to the human race. This gives clear indication that it is within your own individual power to act as you feel you need, and that acknowledging your own individual power becomes terribly important. Not in a way that you can justify but in a way that you can register and pick up on the cellular memory that is contained within the earth itself. And as the earth is trying to feed you what it is receiving from your universe, you begin to wake up and respond.

We acknowledge the discourse of change and the discourse relating to higher consciousness, trying to establish what an 'open mind' means, what greater awareness brings.

This revolution is taking place within your own bodies – not even within your own minds – and as you allow yourselves to become less dense, as you allow the cells within the body to separate very subtly, you allow this memory to establish itself within the cells because the cells can now tolerate it. The Age of Aquarius as your astrologers define it is defined rather well. It is a coming into an age of enlightenment. It is coming into an age of growth and progression. It is allowing you the potential to see. Do understand why, and do try in your own minds to connect, at some point high above you, how you relate to your Animal and Plant Kingdoms. And have a sense of the complementary being that embraces all three in a way that is rather difficult to rationalise and certainly justify. The energy or the consciousness that the earth receives feeds the flora and fauna and you eat the flora and fauna for nourishment, in an unpolluted way. Food, in its natural state, has contained within it a memory that is pure. The more that this food is interfered with chemically, then the more this memory is broken. The closer you can get to eating and drinking what is pure, the clearer your own self-memory and self-relationship will be. The more you allow this food to be contaminated by outside substances, to be converted into 'new food', so you stop remembering, you stop receiving the information from your universe. This brings disharmony and disease because if you stop remembering that the particular vibratory frequencies we talked about earlier no longer exist, you become discon-nected. If you are disconnected, you become lost. Your life becomes aimless. We don't say that going back to the pure essence of food is the solution to your problem but what we are trying to make you aware of is this continuity of vibration that comes through pure food and if you distort it often enough the body will eventually become polluted, clouded.

Somehow the energy connections are not being maintained so that you stop functioning freely and unrestrictedly. Again, this relates very much to the vibration within the body water.

We have talked before about the nature of the fluid surrounding the spine and brain and how it is important that the bone matter is allowed to expand; the spine, the vertebrae, the skull and the bones in the skull are allowed to become more flexible, so that the fluid within the spinal column and indeed the fluid that is contained within the cranial cavity is allowed to flow, with greater ease and unrestriction. This is because, at some point in your future when the bone matter very reluctantly holds itself together, it is this fluid which will become vibrational non-matter, as we mentioned it in our last discourse. Non-matter is not anti-matter, it is merely the next stage beyond the matter state.

Your universe brings a certain cohesiveness to these three specific vibrations and your universe holds these vibrations intact. The stars within your universe act in a completely different way, because the memory contained, or the vibrational nature contained, around these has a greater power, a more direct purpose, and a greater sense of continuity, so that the vibrational influence that each star has on everything contained within your solar system means that on a day-to-day basis it is drawing information from the earth, relaying information back to you about how balance and progression can be maintained. This in turn is related beyond your physical universe. So the stars are fixed points in time. This is so important to remember. The stars are fixed points in time. For us time doesn't exist, so that the stars are fixed points on your five-dimensional graph paper. They relate at very specific points to other very specific points. Your universe merely gives that context. When that context has outgrown its usefulness, it will not longer exist, so that when your science says that the universe was created at one point and is going to reach a point when it will no longer need to exist it is absolutely right. But as scientists relate this to the Big Bang, the Creation and the Big Crunch, the destruction, they are absolutely wrong, because this gives it an importance that it doesn't deserve. Your universe has a certain containment about it, a certain stickiness that allows everything within it to relate well. As you approach this point approximately 2000 years from now, when the human body will start to glow, the whole of your universe will have reached that point of instability where it no longer will be able to contain itself. So it will make that quantum leap into a whole new reality altogether. But it will take with it all the memory and all of the experience that it has already acquired. This will not be lost. It merely becomes something else; if you like, non-matter. It hasn't been destroyed, however, because it was never actually created in the first place, and you can't destroy what hasn't been created, and you can't destroy energy. But as the universe – your universe – will make a whole shift in terms of its consciousness-being, the stars will not. They will continue to act as a reference point, so that as your consciousness evolves and moves to a different set of physical co-ordinates within space, that you acquaint with time, then these stars will remain as they are, as a bridge, to allow consciousness to have directional motion. Once these new co-ordinates have been established by you and your universe, these stars will regroup, acquire a different matter-state that will create vacuums and will draw into this new matter-state fresh density of being. But understand that that density is only density as it relates to what you will be then. We are trying to keep this information as simple as possible so that you can relate to it emotionally. As soon as we try to take this outside of your emotional experience, not only does it become difficult for us to describe, naturally it becomes difficult for you to relate to.

In 2000 years time, therefore, if we look at the three specific vibrations as they relate to the three specific Kingdoms: the Plant, the Animal and the Human, we have a fusion between all three. As matter, as emotional matter then is no longer required, there is no longer a need for distinction between the three. The three become one. If we look at the evolution of different aspects of consciousness within the earth frame over millions of years, this may give you an idea of how complex life-form was when the dense earth vibration initially commenced. And do try to get a sense of the refinement that has taken place through time as you have become more complex. Even the plants have become complex, not in terms of their make-up but in terms of their ability to refine information. This is an interesting concept for you because you may look at a plant that has, possibly, been around for many thousands of years, and you may look at this plant and say: What is different about my relationship to it? I as a human have changed, my species has changed, but the plant has not. Correct. Outwardly it has not, but its ability to absorb, digest and assimilate information has become very complex, because what it is being fed is more complex.

This is also the case within the Animal Kingdom. You look at your species and you say: We must try to save all animal life. Really this isn't practical. It isn't possible. Over the years you will find more and more species running out of time. If you look close enough, you will find more and more cultures within the human species running out of time as well, not only because they have outlived their purpose, but also as you get a blending of blood, a blending of culture, a blending of belief, what eventually you will have will be – we want to say a colour-consciousness – we don't mean this in racial terms but in vibrational terms – what you will have will be a colour-consciousness that embraces all race, all culture and all belief. It is taught, or rather we register other forms of consciousness from our domain communicating with human beings, who talk of seeding, that within the earth there are different races whose own consciousness originates from other different points in space. That is absolutely correct. So that as you experience inter-marriage, within different cultures, what you have in the greater context of matter is a coming together within the blueprint, so that different stars that feed the earth actually come together and that as you come together on earth, certain vibrational bridges are created between the relationships within the star matrix, bringing us to a point when there is total unity of purpose in action. Again, your universe helps make this cohesive and real.

The environment of disappearing species: it is these environments that are naturally under threat. If you examine what these environments represent to you practically as a race, it will be an indication of what you no longer practically require. This can be on land, in your oceans, or in the air. The Animal Kingdom, particularly those who are largely vegetarian, do offer themselves in sacrifice, not out of any sense of pain but out of a sense of duty to create an awareness of what is happening. This is not done to create a sympathetic reaction or to create sorrow, but to create an awareness within the mind – not the heart – of the flexible nature of all life; how it can adapt, regroup, reconstitute itself, become something else. As one life form leaves perhaps another life form enters into the earth that is actually more beneficial and more complementary to your current needs, and, in the process, also creating an awareness of what you're losing emotionally. If we look at the mammals which the human particularly identifies with, as the human is also a mammal, at the dolphin, at the bear, at the whale, you're looking at a life force that is very much reaching a point when its own desire to continue will come to a close. It will leave you at a point when fundamentally there will be only one mammal. This sounds quite dramatic and ruthless. The information is given not necessarily to feel any remorse about what you're destroying, but merely to make you aware also of what you are creating, and what you need to have around you to sustain yourself as you become more flexible, more adaptable and less dependent. As technology will allow you to acquire nourishment from everything that for you is non-natural, what you are heading towards is very much a real place. It has – we have difficulty in explaining accurately – a certain clinical quality or coldness – the closest word we have is – an inanimate quality to it. You will reach a point when you feel: Is there any real need now for us to maintain our role, our emotional state at all? As there will be very little in the earth environment with which you will naturally empathise as empathy will be largely a memory.

Everything within the earth context, metaphorically speaking, is gradually leaving, including you as a race. So understand that through the process of natural progression you will notice plants, animals, certain environments, no longer existing, some of which, yes, you will destroy, some that really have nothing left to contribute. There is a need for you within your own minds to balance this situation so that you can separate what is truly needed from that which really only sustains sentiment. Within your own emotional conditions now you are all finding a need to separate your own state of being from your own emotions – from sentiment – so that you are able to operate more effectively with need, as opposed to desire. Dependency creates desire, which creates obsessive behaviour, which can lead to paranoia if you can't achieve or grasp what it is that you desire. The more that you allow yourselves to separate your state of being from your emotions, the more you are able to understand self in the greater context of the word. Try to put this in perspective with what we have said this evening. Hold that in your hearts, not your minds, and just try and get a sense or a feel for what this means. Allow it to bring to the surface other sensations, because this will eventually bring a certain clarity to what you think and what you believe. Go gently into your own exploration and just be as quietly as you are able – as you are able.

Are there any questions?

*We talked about our universe and that indicates that there are other universes. Is this possible at the same time?*

At the same time – no, this is not possible. Neither is in the same place possible. If we take away the word time and – referring you to your three-dimensional graph paper – as you have particular coordinates which represent your universe, understand that there are many other coordinates that also represent other universes that exist simultaneously. Do you understand the explanation?

*Yes.*

You cannot have two universes in one time. Change the word time to place. You cannot have two different contexts within the same context. If you remove or replace the word 'time' for 'position' and you then look at your piece of graph paper, and you in your time occupy one point, there are many other points surrounding this point on the piece of graph paper, and all of these other points represent different universes, but not within the same time. Conversely, you in your words, cannot exist in their time. In our words, you cannot exist in their place. Your context is different from the other.

*Thank you.*

*Are the stars that you referred to in another place or are they part of our universe?*

This is a very intelligent question. Because of the nature of the stars, yes, they exist in your universe and yes, they exist in other universes as well. Not physically but because of the nature of their consciousness, they are able to relate themselves, replicate themselves, if you like, through different points. So that as you are looking at just a sheet of graph paper, it's like a curve, or a straight line, that has a sense of continuity about it. But again, if we add other dimensions to your piece of graph paper, this means that it relates not linearly but multi-dimensionally. So, yes, they do exist in your time and in your space and also in other times and in other spaces. Does that answer your question?

*Yes.*

*I would like to ask something. Buddhists have a good philosophy about how to liberate the human mind, but they use the same method unchanged for over two and a half thousand years, while you are talking about our evolution and that we will be a completely different species in two thousand years time. Do you have any comment?*

There is no question here apart from an observation. Because something is old, it doesn't mean to say that it isn't new. Just because something has been used for centuries doesn't mean to say that it has no value. You also have to take into consideration the mind, evolving, over the centuries to a point when it cannot contain itself at a superficial level any longer, so that whatever space has been created by Buddhist practice it is now time for others to create that space perhaps in a different way. Or, where there is a dovetailing between what the Buddhists teach and what other people are experiencing for themselves, outside that particular practice. So again, what we have in conclusion, is a coming together or a synthesis of all understanding, all sense of openness and all potential.

*Could you say more about what you mean about need?*

The human cannot isolate itself from the universe. Need is very much unspoken. It is hidden. Need relates to human feeling, the human experience. But need also relates to the spirit and the cosmic. Need relates to exploring what you don't already know. Desire is about possession and ownership. Need is not material. Desire is.

*Do I understand the simple proposition, that certain phases of human existence are obsolete and that this is no cause for alarm?*

Ultimately, yes.

*As humans evolve into a state of non-matter, does this happen gradually as each becomes available to that state or must humanity wait until the last person is ready to evolve?*

It is both and neither. Humanity grows as a whole. This has

to be understood. There is no way in which humanity can grow other than the whole. However, you must appreciate again the speed or the velocity at which this occurs. The greater velocity attained, the greater the collective understanding. The greater the speed, the more that falls by the wayside. So by the time you reach, figuratively, the ultimate speed, you have only got those who can hang on. And once that speed has been acquired, then that potential is present. But you must understand that making that final transformation will be a collective undertaking.

*I'd like to ask something very mundane and practical about water. You were talking about how water carries messages vibrationally and I'm just wondering about the wisdom of continuing to drink tap water every day. I have been told in the past it's a good idea to put a crystal in water, to keep it there for some days before drinking it. Is there anything, in practical terms, you can tell us about water?*

In terms of the human condition in general, you are all very robust, and without major chemical input, you can drink water in quite a polluted state and survive and continue to exist quite well. It really is very much relative to each individual and what you feel you require if, as in your case, there is an increasing sensitivity, both to what you eat and drink and also to those people who surround you. It means that there is a certain refinement coming into your whole energetic environment which almost requires you to refine everything that you bring into your body. This doesn't mean to say that there is going to be any dramatic adverse effect from drinking tap water, but it is very difficult for us to comment. How sensitive do you feel you need to be? How much do you feel you need to remember? How much do you feel you need to make conscious about yourself, even if what you make conscious cannot be practically engaged on a day to day basis in life? Putting crystals in water. Again, each crystal, like a fingerprint, is unique, and has its own particular vibration. So, if you put a crystal in water, you are still subject to what memory is contained within the crystal. You may react to some, you may not to others. You have to take that into consideration. Because the crystal not only amplifies, it also has a refining quality about it, a very particular personality. So again, for you, it means searching for the right crystal that you feel brings the correct vibration to that particular water. But you also have another problem, because as you move about the world, each drop of water that you take in, itself has a different vibration. So as you put that crystal into that particular drop of water, that again will create a different effect. You have to understand that as long as you feel you get nourishment from what you eat and what you drink, as long as you feel that this is comfortable, that is all you need to be aware of. You can become very pre-occupied with the vibratory nature of being. Although we appreciate the intent behind this question, it is difficult for us to advise and say what to do. Your body, in a very crude way, will tell you exactly what you need and what you don't, will alert you very much to what you require, and what you don't, what is appropriate and what is not. And as long as you listen to that in a correct way, there is very little that you will do that will be wrong for you. The message that water carries is again subjected to place. If you are in a particular place, drinking water from that place, there is a certain memory association here. If you move to a different part of the world, again, that memory contained within that water has subjectively a different quality relative to that particular place. Try not to become too sensitive or too precious. Water is a life-giving force. Again, all of you need to reflect on the collective nature, not only of human kind but of all consciousness, and you mustn't lose sight of this unity that is at work.

We draw this evening to a close. Over the coming week, very quietly and very gently, alert yourselves to a vibratory point physically above your head, and try and sense the magnetism that comes from this point as it draws your energy upward. If you can do that, allow yourself to feel what this means. With respect and much love, we adjourn.

# SEVEN

# Nourishment

Conscience can be regarded as responsibility. We know you have heard many times that you're responsible for no-one, but have responsibilities to others. The word responsibility often creates a sense of duty which is, in itself, stressful and limiting, unless that duty relates to your own self-responsibility. If that is the case, how you respond is deeply meaningful. If, however, that duty originates from outside your being, from another person or from an outside situation, it creates an obligation you feel you can't respond to or that you feel is wrong. What's wrong about . it? Responding, even though you feel it's not appropriate? Is that wrong? If that stimulus comes from outside circumstance, there is a certain moral overtone that is often connected with the word duty. This moral overtone suggests that it is very important, indeed vital, that you respond to what this duty represents so that if you feel you shouldn't or don't want to, a guilt process is instigated in your being that creates a sense of paranoia. The paranoia really only represents the confusion between what you sense and what you've been told. Really the conflict between mind and heart. You feel, because feeling is within you. You don't fully realise how feeling is created or why, but it's there. When you feel anything, it stems from you. It relates to your reality. You can't really ignore that, as it is relative to self and truthful by virtue of its very existence. To go against that feeling or intuition can be therefore very detrimental. The signals become confused, the information is contradictory. So not only do we have paranoia, we also have a sense of guilt. The guilt isn't often because of other people or to compensate for other people. It is to compensate for self because of the damage that has been created within self, because an unnecessarily tortured reality has allowed a stimulus from outside to come in. It has taken this on board. It has started to believe in it, even though intuitively it doesn't trust it. The conscience, therefore, is purely self-relative. It is important to understand and stress for yourself that conscience is not to do with response from outside stimulus; it is to do with your being and your relationship with yourself. Nobody can tell you what your conscience says except you. What is your reality? What do you have to learn from that reality? What does the collective have to understand from the response in your reality? And how is that communicated to the universe? Again, you can't look at things in isolation. Ultimately you deal with yourself but beyond that, it is possible to see the ripples that you create within the world. But first of all you have to deal with you, so don't look at the ripples, look at you. Don't look at what you're creating, don't look at the effects that is having in the world. Be and enjoy within the moment of creation itself, because that is perfect. There is no need to try and make it into something else. There is no need to project it into the future because the way for you, the manner in which time is evolving and unfolding, means that there is no way in which you can project that into the future with any sense of consistency or substance.

You're standing on the earth, the earth is round. The earth has no gravity and you fire an arrow hoping that it will land at some other point on the other side of the earth but because of the lack of gravity, it doesn't. It merely proceeds at a tangent away from the earth into space. And that is exactly what your future is about. You standing on the earth. You are used to the gravity. You are used to the attractive forces, the cohesive forces that draw things together. Now that gravity is dissolving, so every action that you take will not necessarily be rooted within your emotional experience. It may have ramifications beyond the earth so you can no longer wait for everything that you do to have an effect within earth-consciousness. It is time to wake up. It is time to realise some of the effects that are being created within you that are permeating the universe itself. It is precisely because of these effects that we have been drawn into physical presence to communicate. That is the motivation. It is yours, more than ours, even though we have motivation too, though not in the same way. Again, we draw your attention to the mirror image of space, of your reality beyond matter, in existence in another situation that is inversely proportional to what you are experiencing now. And that is the other extreme of our reality. That is the other extreme, with which we also work directly. There isn't a polarisation. There isn't a point of non-action or non-happening or non-experience. It is all totally complementary. We know this is difficult for you to entertain, but it is important that you know that it does exist. Why do you create? Why do you work? Why do you feel the need to be active? It is to allow yourselves to emotionally appreciate your being. Now this is very basic. It is fundamental and ultimately limiting, but that is exactly what your emotional reality is about. Which is why you have a spiritual reality as well that is directly involved in emotional experience. So that as you look at your reincarnational cycle you have a life, you have a physical life – in our terms, you have an emotional life. That emotional life dies physically but your consciousness, your whole energy being becomes something else, which is your spiritual reality. That spiritual reality is a place of rest, a place of nourishment, a place of enrichment and also a place of preparation; preparation to return, to act in service, to support, to love, and also to cushion your experience between the emotional and the cosmic. The spiritual actually guides the cosmic as well. It makes the cosmic aware of what it is possible to do. So that your consciousness within the spiritual state has a very broad sense of the universe, has an intimate understanding of subjectivity and objectivity, of empathy and complete detachment.

The spiritual masters, which have before created an energetic web around your emotional being drawing your consciousness into a greater state of awareness of the continuation of all energy force, both scientifically and metaphysically, as they have stepped back have created the potential to make you aware more of detachment. This detachment is purely a device to allow you to let all effect happen without the need to interfere but to observe it and to understand it, so that, as the spiritual observes the emotional enduring this, this knowledge is passed on directly to the cosmic. This allows a greater sense of tangible awareness that has been translated into our language, so we know how to work with you better. It also allows the dimensions, the non-physical dimensions around your earth, to realign themselves more with you. Again using the image of the graph paper, look at three-dimensional graph paper surrounding the earth and then we add fourth and fifth dimensions that are more difficult for you to conceptualise, other dimensions that physically hold the earth in place. You may visualise them as being part of a gigantic hotel that the earth is the core or the middle of, and there are unlimited rooms connecting with each other, surrounding the earth, and these rooms are pockets of energy, forms of consciousness, different spaces, positions in time, and they move, literally, physically move. So collectively, as you respond and become more open or aware of possibility, it does create a physical movement in these other dimensions that surround and hold your earth.

Your science is rather concerned about the earth tilting on its axis, about the change in seasons and the melting of the ice caps. Again this is not arbitrary, but very precise, very direct, and for a very good reason. Not only do we need to look at the redistribution of the population around the earth's surface, we are also looking at the different constitution or composition of the earth's surface itself, between the land and the water, and between what is contained within the land and what is contained within the water. As part of your land becomes unusable and some of your oceans become so highly polluted that they can no longer sustain life in any progressive way, there is a very great need for the earth to shift on its axis to redistribute the vibrational wealth that is already contained within the earth itself, which relates to new micro-organisms being made available to the air which will eventually give rise to the growth of new flora. Then the genetic changes that will take place within the human being will cause a new awareness, not only of what it is possible to eat or drink to sustain yourself, which will bring about a complete revolution in terms of diet, but also of your dependence on flora and fauna, which will become very different. Your reliance on the flesh of animals, of fish, of micro-organisms, as that becomes less and less, you will learn to derive nourishment in a more fundamental, elemental way.

It is difficult for us to describe without creating alarm, but your becoming aware of the elemental nature within the earth itself could mean deriving energy from crystals, deriving energy from primitive earth. But, again, remembering that as the physical body increases its vibration over a period of time, you cease to assimilate nourishment from any hydrocarbon that has a dense vibrational being. So being able to assimilate nourishment, for example, from pure elements such as carbon, potassium, molybdenum, silicon, magnesium and even strontium (which may perhaps seem odd as it is slightly radioactive). But literally, in a very crude way, being able to eat your earth will become a distinct possibility. We mean this more in terms of deriving energy from crystalline-form directly rather than the need to survive off the living organism. Within your own physical being, there is a certain crystalline quality that the physical body is endeavouring to attain, so that when the ultimate moment arrives and you start to glow, fundamentally what we have is pure crystalline composition which then feeds off light itself. So the ability to transform that light into energy and transmute it into a whole new state of being can be very real indeed. There is a build-up within volcanic matter of precisely this, mineral contents, micro-organisms that are going to come to the surface more and more, giving you a whole variety and range of other life-forms which will, in future time, give sustenance in a way that you haven't always experienced. So that when you look, in a linear way, at the destructive forces of nature, what you have is these raw, inner, elemental forces working in co-operation in a very complementary way, eroding what is no longer required, and bringing to the surface exactly, and in a very precise way, what is required.

We are aware of communication from many different sources arising in various parts of the world, of living in the earth, under the earth, living under sea, indeed living under earth under sea, and that there are beings, consciousness forms, under the earth, which can sustain life and which can instruct and can give a progressive sense of Being; this Being seen both as a metaphor and as an actual reality. Do know that the possibility of this is becoming less of a metaphor and that the consciousness that is contained within the crystalline formation within the earth itself, will be made more widely known. That you will literally be physically instructed as to how to use these forms of consciousness and nourishment, and that you will very deliberately go into and under the earth and under the oceans to receive this instruction. Although this may sound rather bizarre, this is how it will be. It does not mean to say that you relinquish living on the surface of the earth. It doesn't necessarily mean that you lose a need to respire, but the relationship between earth and the air, as that becomes measurably different, so the way that you draw your life force from air and earth, will also become different.

Understand that a new land-mass will come to the surface east of the eastern seaboard of the United States and South America. Also, north east of Indonesia there will be a resurfacing of another significant land-mass that will give rise to a whole new vibratory state within the earth itself. This will be an emergence or a resurfacing of a totally different crystalline energy, that is physically tangible and measurable, and that is going to cause a distinct shift in the awareness-creating ability of individuals within the earth. It will mean that certain places within the surface of the earth become uninhabitable, as the vibrations there are unsustainable. So, looking at the distribution of the population around the earth, it will mean that it will be drawn to these new places of existence over a period of time, when they begin to recognise the physical wealth and the vibrational wealth that they both have to offer. When this sort of resurgence establishes itself, the major cities of the world as they are now will cease to become habitable, only because the desire to be in those places will be diminished, rather than there being any physical destruction. It will have more to do with the emanation coming from these new land-masses and the resulting streams of consciousness that flood into the earth plane. This will mean that only a select few will want to remain in cities and only for very particular reasons; reasons mainly connected with control, power and dependency, and the inability to move away from the controlling influences of the emotional being.

The north and western seaboards of Australia, New Zealand as it moves across the southern oceans, Indonesia, beyond the west coast of Ireland, around the Azores, around the north western seaboard of Canada, south towards Hawaii, are all going to become points of crisis. There is no other word for the sort of change that is going to take place within these areas. They are significant points, they are very reactive points, but they are also points of dynamic growth and this must not be forgotten. In spite of the natural destructive power, the effect that these points will encounter will be enormous and it may be perceived that this is Armageddon, this is the end of the world. Is the upsurge in activity within these points of the globe going to cause such an instability in terms of the rotation of the earth on its axis, or its physical position within the solar system, that it is actually going to send the solar system out of balance? Yes, this is the case. Again, I refer you to what we said earlier about the earth, and indeed the solar system, being contained within this enormous hotel which has within it many rooms, that physically hold the earth and solar system within its grasp. Because of the flexibility and the movement contained within these rooms, no matter what reverberation takes place in and around the earth and the solar system, this other inter-dimensional, multi-dimensional hotel can actually hold all in a very real and stable manner, nothing is 'out-of-control'. There is no destruction. It is merely the universe flexing its muscles and getting a sense of its own power. You merely respond as you need to at that point in time. Do not concentrate on the effect of this happening but understand more the purpose of why it has happened in the first place, relating to your own consciousness change, your own physiological and physical structure adapting through time. If you take a moment to marry that with the very dramatic changes within the earth's surface itself and the composition of the earth and what it brings to the surface, then, as the earth becomes crystalline, so do you. As you increase your vibration, so does the earth. And the reciprocal relationship that you have with each other is not only intimate but direct. Spend time reflecting on this, and allow those concepts just to be within you. Try not to make them into anything. As these concepts resonate within you, they will bring to the surface certain awareness and understanding, certain other concepts, allowing you to belong to them more, in a more forgiving way, so that there is less need to delineate or justify. And allow your heart, as a result, to give yourself all the understanding you need. It's like the stroking of spirit on the top of the head that brings about a greater sense of relaxation within self, within being, within all that is.

Are there any questions?

*Yes. Some people are observing coloured lights on people's skins. What is the significance of this?*

It does relate very directly to the crystalline nature of your physiological being establishing itself. Within cellular memory (it is difficult to describe this as it hasn't been observed, it hasn't been physically measured), what you have is your physiological being utilising light, physical light, in a totally different way. Why is your ozone layer decreasing? Why is the ultra-violet frequency having a stronger hold and influence in your reality? Why are those x-rays, which are rather dense in formation, able to permeate the surface of the earth with greater frequency? Again, your ability to hold – no, excuse me, the words aren't always appropriate – to absorb and reflect light is increasing. The properties of the skin become activated in a new way, as the moisture or the water content in the subcutaneous levels are able to vibrate at a higher level. It is as though minute crystals are placed under the skin so that, as you see sunlight passing through a prism, you see many different colours. There is an absorption process going on here and a reflective one, which draws in the light but also reflects many different colours within that spectrum of light. So it is within the properties of those subcutaneous levels of skin within the body and, as previously mentioned, about the property of water and the memory contained within water. Now if we marry the memory-property of the water itself with the memory-property within DNA, and we look at the cooperative nature of these two hidden memories and how those memories are suddenly becoming more readily available, it explains perhaps in a more tangible way what we are talking about in terms of crystalline substance in the earth becoming more active, and the body itself becoming a unity of that sort of crystalline energy. You will see this more and more. Part of the marriage, or the mixing of blood and culture on the earth, in extreme, brings together the white and the black, the pale and the dark, so that ultimately there is a unity of colour. This unity of colour, in vibrational terms, allows the human being to be more tolerant – in very simple terms – of the sun, and all of the rays that exist within the universe as they interact with the earth itself. The purpose is to bring about unity, to bring about endurance, so that flexibility of being can be continually experienced and explored. Is this helpful to your question ?

*Yes, thank you.*

*There are two notions which, at the moment, puzzle me a little bit as regards our everyday life. One is the need to open our heart to one ability, which is to experience, and the other is the need for an ability toward detachment, to see feelings as merely accompanying our experience.*

If you regard the heart as your unconditional being, your ability to appreciate everything becomes much greater. When we talk about detachment, we talk of detachment from lower feeling and lower sensation. Human love is lower feeling, lower sensation. This is not to bring this into the level of bathos. It is not to diminish the importance of love, but when we look at the nature of the unconditional heart that makes accessible divine love, giving you an uncomplicated relationship with your unconditional self, then that is what we mean by opening the heart. Try not to justify. We continually repeat this. Try not to justify your own present reality and equate it with what we say. Your reality is important for you to experience. The way that we describe things often doesn't relate to what you understand in terms of feeling and emotion. It is difficult for us to make an apology for this as we understand immediately the difficulty this sort of communication creates but as long as you hold the difference within your being between the unconditional, which is unlimited, and the emotional, which is limited, you have your answer.

As we bring to a close a spontaneous happening of two very different states of being, do know that all of you present now begin to hold part of our vibratory nature within your realm of existence. We are aware that some of you have experienced some discomfort within the situation of our encounters and this does bear a relationship with your contact with this often dispassionate vibratory state. In time to come, this vibration will allow you to tolerate circumstance and allow you to maintain a perspective which, once, in retrospect, may have seemed impossible. Hold this in your mind, and continue to be alert to you and your resourcefulness. What is given is given because it is deserving, and the integrity with which this vibrational being will be introduced and assimilated by you will be progressively more under your command in a more fully conscious way. Until the next time.

# EIGHT

# The Veils of Being

We wish to discuss the 17 veils of vibratory being. For us, there exist 17 different stages in which consciousness opens itself up to experience, to allow progressive understanding to rule, so that over a period of time the collectivity of experience and information can bring about resolution. We see this not only in terms of your emotional, spiritual experience, but also in terms of matter and non-matter. We will endeavour, in a rather crude way to make you aware of these different stages.

First, we have origin; the point when consciousness becomes individual. Look at collectivity, the collective unconscious, or universal consciousness. One day an aspect breaks away from this unified force, and this aspect moves through space. It can fragment, it can remain singular, and let us say that this aspect is you. Within origin there is an impulse – as a human being you would call this need – to explore and understand. How can you possibly want to understand when, while being complete within the collective unconscious, you have an appreciation of all? This is a mystery which, for the moment, will remain a mystery. But an impulse is created to leave, causing the aspect to journey, and to choose what environment it wishes to experience. So the aspect, when it leaves the point of origin, has a choice as to what place and what time it wishes to surface and become a part of. So, even at the point of origin, there is choice. Even before origin was created, there was a choice as to whether you became part of origin. To understand what creates is the most difficult to convey comprehensively as we ourselves perceive this within limited light as well as you.

Origin brings you to the second point, which is experience and experience dictates the third point context. As we look at experience, it allows the aspect to have genuine choice as to what it feels it requires to experience. This choice is genuine. But even within the point of origin, the motivation that creates the separation of the aspect from itself, to leave home as it were, has already given that aspect a quality that will cause it to be magnetised to a certain place. Even though there is this genuine choice, the aspect is likely to be magnetised towards an experience which is naturally attractive to it. So already, within the point of ultimate origin, there is within the aspect – namely you – an impulse that is going to direct you in a very particular way. The experience of this then redefines the aspect in such a way that allows it to choose place.

The third; context. Context, within place, allows the aspect to choose with greater precision the dimension within place.

Dimension is the fourth aspect. The fourth veil. Looking at your five dimensional piece of graph paper, once the aspect is drawn in to a particular coordinate, there is an expansion within that coordinate, so that although there is a certain precision about this place, you are then given the opportunity to look at dimension. So let us examine dimension, the fourth veil. Even within a particular co-ordinate, for example earth, the solar system and your universe, there are dimensions around you. The emotional, the spiritual, the cosmic. Matter, non-matter, anti-matter. Parallels, contra-parallels. Even within the very precise nature of your experiential being, there are counter-realities, counter-places, which are difficult to define. So within this fourth veil, crudely speaking, we look at whether the experience of matter or anti-matter is most important. Matter and non-matter. As you move into matter, it creates a density around the consciousness that profoundly alters the trajectory of your being; causes you to totally re-assess the impulse and the motivation, bringing stronger clarity and focus to experience.

The fifth veil is matter, and this is the dimension in which you choose to experience. As you come into matter, the density of the energy surrounding the aspect or the incoming consciousness, namely you, acquires the frequency that sets it apart from others. It gives it a sense of 'specialness'. So here we have greater precision coming into place, coming into time, that defines your consciousness very particularly indeed, and this is the first opportunity for us to relate to you as conscious human beings. It is not here at the fifth veiled point that this occurs. So just at a very simple level, there are many processes that you are involved with before your consciousness, your soul, your spirit, what you represent, comes into a point of existence which becomes even remotely specialised in any way. Having chosen matter, you then – along your line of trajectory – choose qualitative experience. It causes you to choose what physical universe to surface within.

The sixth veil is universe. The sixth veil offers containment. The sixth veil is the first time where there is noticeable specialisation within the emotional make-up of your being. This is not an accurate description of you, as you as yet have not acquired an emotional personality, but it is a point where the consciousness acquires a gaseousness, a certain density, a certain luminosity, that can define you in measurable terms from other forms of consciousness. So you have now chosen your universe, which brings us to the point of all the previously explored items of discussion. We are now at base. We stand outside your universe, we see it, we observe it, and this is the beginning of you, the identifiable you, as you emotionally relate to it. Within universe, you then choose whether to be part of emotional experience, or whether to co-operate outside of emotional experience. In the words that we use, you choose whether to be spiritual or cosmic.

The seventh veil is density. Density defines again how this gaseous state is going to be confined, and as consciousness comes into density, it allows it to appreciate more the initial motivation that it had when it left the point of origin. This is the point when the instinctive memory within the consciousness understands how it is cooperating with the absolute.

The eighth veil concerns position and direction. Position relates to the point of experience within the universe, your universe. The position you choose is your galaxy. Within this galaxy you have the familiar constellations which are visible to the human eye, and you have your solar system. Welcome to the real, emotional context. Within this context you are giving yourself over to real experience where you forfeit freedom of physical movement.

Moving on to the next veil, the ninth; emotional

compaction. Here there is a real commitment to the compression of molecules. Here is where consciousness memory becomes formalised in such a way that it loses its first sense – let us rephrase this. It loses its sense of its point of origin, as it commits to life experience.

The tenth veil is the human condition, where you experience acute limitation. You lose your memory. You become ignorant and inward looking. You involve yourself in perpetual experience which brings you to a point when you gain sufficient understanding of this dense nature of being so that you then become free from it. Free then to experience what is beyond the tenth veil. There is a subdivision within the tenth veil which concerns your spiritual being. Previously we have talked about the emotional and the spiritual as being part of the same context, that really they are only mirror images of each other. Although there is no physical density within the spiritual, although there is no emotional empathy here, there is a direct understanding of what this means, so that when the consciousness moves in and out of physical and spiritual being, there is a total understanding of what this represents. So the spiritual being is contained very much within the tenth veil.

The eleventh veil is enlightenment, that point when consciousness explodes into a glowing light form which lights up the reality within your solar context. This creates a reverberation within the solar context that frees the planets, that frees human consciousness from its own chains and allows it to progress. Within this context, there is an expansion towards righteousness. This word has no moral value as you normally interpret this within your psychological state. This righteousness has a direction and purpose which redirects towards the source, or guides the enlightened consciousness in a way that will eventually reach the point where it can fuse once more with the ultimate being.

The next veil, the twelfth, is coherence. This is not an accurate description of what happens. The word doesn't truly represent the unification of consciousness, as it has experienced the earthly condition with itself beyond the emotional condition. What we have is a certain separation within itself that allows it to lose a protective layer. That protective layer was in place for the human consciousness to be defended, if you like, by any form of vibratory consciousness which could be construed as being destructive or creating such a high frequency that would be intolerable for the emotional condition. So at this point of coherence it is moving beyond the spiritual, moving beyond the emotional altogether and leaving it behind. Leaving it open to experience the universe once more in an unadulterated fashion.

The next veil, the thirteenth, concerns velocity. Velocity relates less to speed and more to synthesis, becoming more what it is not. Again, this is difficult for us to describe, but look at the possibility of consciousness becoming non-matter, anti-matter or going into other dimensional states of being in a different place other than where they have had emotional experience. This is what we mean. So that synthesis allows consciousness the opportunity to enter into a neutral position where nothing happens. Synthesis into everything where nothing happens.

The next veil, the fourteenth, is credibility. Again, the word is not an accurate reflection of what is happening here, but it gives you an indication, an emotional indication, of what that consciousness is to experience. Having moved into synthesis, it then allows it to deliberate, to understand how it can support what it has already experienced within the framework of time and space, while being loyal to that experience in a way that gives progressive understanding to those other forms of consciousness that haven't experienced the emotional condition. This is where the credibility fits in. Experience, in your language, has integrity. The more widely experienced the consciousness is, the greater voice it can have through all time and space. The level of your experience within the earthly context gives your being a credibility that has a very loud voice within all universes, which is why there are many forms working with you now to maintain balance, harmony and progression. Credibility, then, within the consciousness state, allows you to define your voice, not find your voice, but to define it. To choose how you will use this consciousness experience in a progressive way allows you to move into the next veil, the fifteenth.

This veil is supra-dimensional being. We are coming close to the end. Supra-dimensional: living above or beyond dimension. How can it be possible to live above dimension? To live above dimension suggests that you are no longer part of any reality whatsoever, as we have tended to define all of your experience within this five-dimensional graph paper. But do understand, that doesn't mean to say that you have to live within it. It doesn't mean to say that you have to experience within it. Suspend your disbelief, understand that anything is possible, and while most experience is about being contained within particular co-ordinates within all time space, appreciate also that it is possible to live outside of all containment. Supra-dimensional being gives you a sense of objectivity that allows you to see everything. It allows you to appreciate everything. It is living beyond law, beyond restriction, beyond compaction. This is the point when wisdom becomes knowledge, where all experience, where all understanding acquires a critical density that takes it beyond the need to experience. Surely this only belongs to God, you say. But understand, as you are now very close to what 'all that is' represents, then yes, you are part, a very close part, of what that ultimate 'all God is' is for you. Again, not in the personified sense, but in the sense of all being, all consciousness, all. Supra-dimensional being also allows you to communicate directly with other forms of consciousness so that your experience can be valued in a directional way. 'Supra' does not mean that you are beyond communicating experience, even though it means that you are beyond experience, so there is still purpose here. You haven't sacrificed experience altogether. You haven't allowed yourself to be totally set apart. There are certain energy channels that continually remain open, and the objectivity that comes from this state of being has such an unconditional presence within all time-space that its value cannot possibly be under-estimated.

The next, sixteenth, veil brings us to light fusion. Please be liberal in your interpretation of this. This level of being is not necessarily dense enough to emanate light. It is difficult for us to explain, but it is the essence of light rather than light itself. Within this there is a certain matrix and this matrix governs about 40% of all reality. It would not be inaccurate to say that at this veil we have motivation for all light, that all light emanates from this state of being and that this light goes through all matter, all non-matter, all forms that have experienced matter and non-matter, and all forms that support that whole contained experience.

The penultimate, which is also the ultimate veil, relates to pulse. In a crude way you could interpret this as being vibration, frequency, friction. Wherever pulse chooses to experience can bring about a harshness or a density of experience that brings about resolution. Understand resolution isn't always purposeful, that there are some states where there is no resolution, there is merely experience. The experience of certain places or spaces means that to enter into that place is enough, that there is nothing to resolve; there is nothing to understand. There is merely something to experience. When we look at the pulse we are looking at the origin of vibratory being altogether. Again, this governs approximately 40% of all that is, so the pulse in combination with the light permeates all experience, all non-being, all dimensions. We say this is the ultimate as there is only one state beyond this, but in many ways there is no state beyond this. To say that you return to your original source is not entirely accurate as you left your point of origin and so ultimately you are to return. You get so close but never close enough that now friction has been created, or now motivation towards experience has been created, that there is no going back to total balance, to total stillness, to total beingness. This may be a difficult concept to hold as surely you think we reach a point of exactness or purity where we can once more blend with the ultimate source. But do understand that as a motivation has been created for the aspect of consciousness to move away from the source, it allows you to return, circulate and be a part of the source without being part of the source, and in your terms, the desire to be part of the source again means that you become the source. This is also a concept that is difficult for us to fully appreciate. At our level of understanding it is not possible for us to become part of the source once more. There is a gap of experience here in the ratio of 20%. This 20% creates a safety-valve where the source itself has direct access to all. Comparing the ratios of the 80% to the 20%, in a very crude way, means that all the different aspects of consciousness have a greater proportion than the God-source, and in many ways, this is entirely accurate. But as the 80% has lost the God-source, it allows it the freedom to remain apart or separate as well as giving it the potential to understand as much as the God-source itself. So there's a sense of living in harmony with the God-source with an experience of everything through all time, through all place, through all dimensional being, that gives it a greater expansion than the God-source itself. But you must also understand that there is such a sense of purity contained within the God-source, that it doesn't require that experience for it has within it a certain active quality that doesn't need it to react. It is difficult to explain this in ways that you can appreciate. Let us explain it in another way. Being in the position of being capable of creating and destroying means that often neither is required because there is a total understanding of each. The level of intelligence is such that there is perfect balance, perfect harmony. There has been no experience of imbalance or disharmony which makes it perfect and that is the difference between the 20% or the God-source and the 80% which in many ways has experienced more than the God-source, but having left the God-source, it has chosen to experience rather than to be but the resonance between the 80% and the 20% within itself brings about a sense of dynamic inaction that is perfect in its own right allowing it to be in total balance, total harmony, total resonance, giving itself namely the 80%, the opportunity to re-experience, should that be required or desired.

To sum up: within the 20%, there is nothing to prove as there is total understanding so there is total being. Within the 80% it has experienced, it has understood, there is a certain completeness, a totality of being. But the manner of acquiring that totality of being is very different as effect has been involved, as proof has been experienced, bringing it to a state of equal balance, equal harmony, equal peace. But they are different. They are unique, and they are both the same.

Reflect on the veils. Don't pay too much detailed attention to the words that we used to describe the veils. They are not always accurate, but we do try to give you something that you can relate to emotionally. But within these different stages see that you are only one stage, which will give you some idea of your insignificance, of your tiny position within everything. But do understand that, within your own particular veil, this experience is being acquired in a way that does not exist anywhere else. It is unique to you. So despite the insignificance, the magnitude of this is unique. It is important, therefore, to realise how small you are, yet how special the emotional and spiritual experience is for all of human kind and all realities as they inter-relate with each other. You do choose this with precision, even though it is God-given. To separate will from desire becomes very difficult. To say whether you have ultimately free-will is very difficult, as the motivation you draw into yourself (namely the aspect of consciousness when it originally leaves the source), means that you already accept something that takes you into experience, which suggests there isn't free-will here at all, as, from the moment that you accept that motivation into your consciousness, you are responding rather than initiating. However, there was a choice to respond, but there was an initiation, there was a beginning. Do not try, within your framework of existence to justify free will. There is no real answer to this. You cannot allow your minds to concep-tualise what this represents. You have to acknowledge to yourself that yes, I do have free will, and within the circum-stance of your reality, indeed you do. But merely reflect this through time and space, through all dimensions. And just to get a sense of the enormity of the concept of original-being and ultimate-being, so that, to understand the difference, you follow the ellipse of that experience through space back to the point of origin. Ultimately there is no separation but there is a difference. Ultimately there is only one reality, one way in which to be.

Reflect on being. We can't stress how important it is. As you reflect on being, it opens you up to inter-dimensional experience. This may not make any rational sense as you allow yourself to open in this way. But the energy shock that resonates through you does create a degree of inter-connectivity between you and what is else; that does leave a lasting fingerprint on your being, that does allow you to belong more – to what, we can't say, as it isn't specialised in that way. But do understand that, as that being explodes and opens, it simulates your belonging. It reaffirms your 'is-ness', and allows security of being to become a more tangible conscious possibility, as you move towards dwelling within your own house of divine self.

We leave you merely with a concept, a concept to focus and explode your reality into nothing, where everything is possible.

This evening's encounter may leave you with an empty mind and a feeling of dissociation. Do not allow this to alarm you in any way, it is merely to prepare you for what is to come and allow you to understand more your unconditional nature, as what is given is always given with love, pulsing with light, to stimulate. With a smile – until the next time.

# NINE

## *Kundalini*

We draw the being of your vessel into a deep, tranquil space that is like darkest night. In this space your vessel experiences nothing but calm; physical calm and emotional calm. What is heightened as he goes into this space is an awareness of the energy contained within the spine. If you look at a medieval sword which has as the blade the area of the spine below the shoulders; as the guard, the cross that goes above the shoulders; and the grip which represents the head, then you see what he sees. We activate this symbol which, for him, represents spiritual strength and cosmic glory. This sword is burning hot and can't be touched but can be experienced, and this sword within him lays not dormant, passively, but is entirely active. This means that there is always a stage of preparation, even though this sword may not always be used either to attack or to defend. For him, defence does not exist, so the reality of this sword only means that he will use it to attack. To attack is to cut through truth and to look through the essence. The sword at this moment is passively active or actively passive. The point is aimed towards the ground but there is a sense of alertness contained within it which means that it is alert to truth, to wisdom and to understanding, and it vibrates at a frequency that allows us to have a voice. In attack mode it means that the strength contained within this will have expression. The strength that is contained here has not, as yet, had an expression but the strength is there for him to draw on when or if the time is appropriate.

We wish to talk about the nature of Kundalini and your understanding of this in relation to the spiritual context and the cosmic reality, so that you are able to have a perspective on what it represents in its own right in terms of progressive experience. Kundalini has been taught within earth-consciousness as a spiritual force that can transform. In many ways alchemy, as it is represented or understood by the philosophers, is what Kundalini is about: transforming the physical into the spiritual while that remains contained within the physical body, so that we are not looking for actual gold, we are looking for the cosmic gold being contained or transformed within the physical body. This allows that individual to be able to hold within themself potential for all understanding. This doesn't mean that that individual understands everything but the potential for that individual to have access to everything is very real indeed. So you do not look to your vessel for understanding of everything, but know that that vessel has the potential realised to reach or not to reach into everything and to be able to draw from it whatever is relevant at that time. It is the relevant part which is important because, even though the potential is there to draw upon everything, it doesn't mean to say that it is wise to do it.

He struggles to find a way to express what he understands but he also understands that there is no need to express what is already present and that is the frustration, because within him there is already an awareness of what is possible, and that can't be voiced or put into words – that understanding is present. The frustration that he feels is knowing this consciously but also knowing consciously that there is no need to vocalise what only needs to be understood. The frustration is merely emotional, and the frustration is an expression, within the spiritual realms, of what is beyond its need to experience and what is beyond its need to communicate. So there is a double frustration if you like, not only at an emotional level but also at a spiritual level.

We talk about this in relation to your vessel to give you some understanding of the progressive nature of the Kundalini and what it represents through the history of your time. The transformative power of the Kundalini has historically vaulted evolved souls into the realm of spiritual understanding and appreciation that allows them to teach, that has allowed them to communicate, and allowed them to give voice to what they were unable to say previously. Historically, it has been connected to enlightenment, to heightened awareness, to having certain psychic gifts or insightful powers, stimulating intuition and laying bare instinct in a vulnerable manner, so that there is no way in which an individual can avoid seeing or experiencing what it represents. It makes an individual, or has made an individual, more visible to others, seemingly against their will and given them a focus that consciously they didn't always choose. But having been catapulted into a level of awareness, they often feel that what has to be communicated outweighs any reticence or anxiety which previously inhibited them from doing so. We create what has already been said in relation to the spiritual and the cosmic context, but as we move through time, you have reached a point – now – where the whole context of life, the waking state of the mind, and what it is prepared to entertain as understanding becomes crucially vulnerable. You ask, you know not what for, and you accept and acknowledge the response to what you ask for. Again there may not be a conscious awareness of what that is, but merely an exchange of energy. This is important. Over a period of time, this energy builds up to a critical point, where it makes a quantum leap into a new area of understanding. The rules of science dictate that this is how it has to be. Spiritual law and the laws of Karma suggest that, as you move through time, the critical accumulation of experience brings you to a point of non-experience, when you are eventually free from your need purely to understand the human context through the emotional condition. This is when real freedom asserts itself. This leaves you at a point of non-experience and pure potential, so that what you have then, figuratively speaking, is no knowledge and complete understanding. No desire for knowledge, but a thirst to be able to receive that which is beyond your consciousness.

Kundalini, by its very nature, has evolved through time. Kundalini should not be consciously evoked, although we understand that ways to evoke it are taught. Spontaneity relative to individuals and their own spiritual growth is important in the way that it creates a fusion between the two. To artificially stimulate this only means that there will be a gap between the emotional maturity and that emotional being being able to sustain any awareness that comes with the evocation of the Kundalini energy. This lack of maturity can bring about all sorts of problems within your emotional context. From madness, losing control of the mind process altogether, to feeling that you will never, or can never, apply yourself. Suddenly the emotional context, your earthly experience doesn't mean anything. It is necessary to have this fusion of body, mind and spirit in such a way that suddenly there is no separation (even though ultimately there is no separation) but so that consciously, within your emotional being, you do not delineate or separate the operation of the emotions from that of the mind and that of the spirit.

The spontaneous eruption of this energy takes human consciousness beyond the human condition. It gives an overview, it gives an objectivity that allows you to be a part of the human race while being separate from it. This doesn't necessarily mean that you're special, but it allows the individual to maintain individuality without separation. It allows the individual to decide consciously how much they want to be part of the human race. It also allows, within this detachment the Objective Being to invite into itself whatever progressive reality is close to it. This is terribly important within the context of what we are about to say. As you specifically move through time and figuratively leave the spiritual context behind more and more, as it becomes less relevant, the opening of that cosmic door – so that the blueprint of information is made more freely available – means that potentially you can bring into your being cosmic elements which your emotional body would not have previously been able to hold within it vibrationally.

We talked in our last meeting about the many different stages of consciousness, as we perceive them. Without trying to remember what was said, as the Kundalini explodes within the individuals in your present time (and your present time, in reality, started approximately 36 months ago) it means that these different veils of consciousness can now be raised for those who have Kundalini experience. This doesn't mean to say everybody that has these Kundalini experiences will have free access to these veils of consciousness, but more and more people will. So that their ability to understand, their ability to have an energy exchange with those 17 veils, becomes tangible. When that exchange of energy takes place and you have people around your globe waking up in this way, they will literally hold a funnel of energy. This inter-dimensional mechanism that allows them, on your behalf, to hold this cosmic radioactive force within the parameters of your emotional earth life can then transmit, subliminally, information to all those who are receptive.

Don't think about what we have just said, just allow its reverberation to enter into your being. We have talked earlier of the constitutional composition of your bodies. If you regard Kundalini as an injection of radioactive material into the base of the spine which creates an instability, you have the picture exactly. The constitution of the body will depend on whether that individual is able to maintain an experience of this nature. There is a strengthening of the metallic element or makeup of every individual within this room, and as this metallic makeup becomes more resilient, it will very subtly change the physiological functioning within your body. You notice this as we have said before most clearly in terms of diet, in terms of mood swings, and in terms of sensitivity. But do understand that as the metallic composition within the body is stressed, the radiation that comes from the body is increased, which allows it to synthesize directly with the metallic composition within the earth, which in turns creates a reaction throughout all space, which allows you inter-dimensionally to draw on this elemental quality through all time and space. The further out into your solar system – and indeed into your universe – that this extends, the greater stability will be ultimately felt, even though the process of physiological change will create some discomfort, but do understand that you, as an individual, are setting up a reverberation through all space that allows you to feel your place within the cosmos. There is no real rational explanation of it as your experience is purely intuitive. The effect of this helps hasten the crystallisation within the water properties of the physical body. We have already talked of this at length. A question was asked about the colour emanation within the skin. Those of you who are experiencing this must understand that it is in direct response to the strengthening of the metallic qualities within the body. You become, in a crude way, more highly magnetised. This causes you to use up the energy reserves in your body more quickly, which will create a drain on the vitamin and mineral quality within the body. As we have said, it will also create quite a deal of stress, on the physical skeleton and the bone composition, which will start to become less cohesive. As you move into old age there may be some experience of degenerative bone disease. You are not to be alarmed by this. Again, as we look at the context of your evolving consciousness through time, through matter, you must also remember that you don't always experience the effect of any impulse within the space of one lifetime, so the accumulative understanding can occur in another time, in another place.

As there is a strengthening of this magnetic resonance within the body, it prepares Kundalini Energy for recognition. You may find in one lifetime that you come very close to having a Kundalini experience where the awareness is ripe to be expanded, but then as you hold this magnetic resonance more comfortably within your body, it takes away the pressure from the evocation of the Kundalini and postpones it. It is possible to postpone this evocation completely, as you draw information and understanding through your own cellular memory which doesn't require this alchemy within the physical body. So what we have is the body evolving through time and space to a point when there won't be a need for this Kundalini expression at all. But there is another mechanism, if you like, in place, that will allow you to draw on this awareness in a completely different way. As each cell eventually becomes a composite crystal, the resonances that will reverberate within your being, are enough to maintain elevated thought and motivation without the need for the physical disturbance that comes with Kundalini experience. Being born with the Kundalini already risen is also a prospect that you need to entertain. Within the spiritual realm a sense of fusion can be attained, so that when the incoming consciousness enters into the physical body there is no need for the Kundalini to be released at all.

It is also important to remember that the Kundalini experience happens only once in your evolvement through time; that if you regard this as an energy-force which allows you to be a projectile hurled through space, the added momentum only needs to be given once. The speed, metaphorically speaking, which is given to that evolving consciousness, can hasten its arrival at the point of spiritual (we don't have a word for it), spiritual ultimatum, spiritual destination, where there is nothing further for the spiritual to communicate through the spiritual body. Then there is a total release of everything that is emotional. There is a total release of emotional Karma. The laws that govern that particular reality become obsolete. The particular individual then becomes absorbed into a higher framework of being, one that will remove it from the earth context altogether.

It has been recorded and spoken that those who have this particular experience feel that they have been brought close to God. What they mean is they experience the purity of their own being, the true and unadulterated nature of their unconditional being in such a way that they are in no doubt of their divinity; of the presence of divinity itself, of the pervasiveness of an unconditional love that regulates all. To experience that is the ultimate for the human being, as there is nothing beyond that experience which is relevant. Bearing this in mind, as you move through time, as you reach the point when you no longer have a need for density of being and that the crystal cells within the body separate in such a way that you glow purely of light, that is the point when there is no need for Kundalini. As you become light, as the difference between your emotional body and your spiritual body becomes one, there is total fusion, and as that fusion takes place, you become neither, for the need to experience in that way again is obsolete. Being catapulted into the cosmic reality makes people collectively aware of being able to live outside of empathy.

In many ways, for the human to think that they don't need to empathise is a rather incongruous concept. Not having to join in, although it offers opportunity, creates anxiety as people often feel that they are losing touch with reality, losing touch with the basis of feelings, as they often feel that if they let go of desire, that desire is no longer a motivating force within their life. Perhaps desire then fuses completely with need. At that point there is no separation from what is required of you and what you feel you have to achieve. This is important. Your life is about feeling you Have To Do, feeling you Have To Accomplish. To take that away would almost make life seem pointless, and so it would be. You don't stop creating the goals, but as you approach those goals, your understanding of what they represent becomes more and more complete, which means perhaps you don't have to achieve. The expectation leaves your life. There is no longer anything to depend on.

Kundalini brings the waking mind into a state beyond experience. Again this is a very difficult concept for your conscious minds to hold onto. How can you be in a point beyond experience? Just for a moment let that resonate within your being. How can you be at a point beyond experience? Subjectively, it may not fit within your brain. This may not compute. Perhaps somewhere within your being there is a chord of recognition which can be satisfied with no logic. To be at a point beyond experience means that you are allowing yourself to be drawn into the void of all. There is no preparation. There is merely recognition of where you are at any given point in time. And this empty space, within which is everything, allows you to exchange energy with everything. As you draw that energy into your being, it simulates the energy at the base of the spine where the Kundalini lives. That energy stirs itself. There is a reverberation up into the spine, and the reverberation hits the cerebral cortex, which brings about a sense of recognition. Brings about a recognition of belonging where you have no notion or idea, but that recognition feeds back the energy to the base of the spine which says, peace now. We understand the impulse. We know what you are trying to say. What are you trying to say? As long as you allow yourself to be free to experience, there is nothing else you need to aim for. The Kundalini is being provocative in a way that allows you to be, and allows you to believe in nothing. These are merely the fruits of its existence. By showing you how futile objectives are, you do reach a point where you stop creating them.

That is the point when spontaneity of being is realised. This brings us back to what we were explaining earlier. That with some there will be no need to experience this Kundalini surge through the physical body. People experience the release of this Kundalini through the whole of their life. Some people feel it over a period of years, some weeks, some days, some instantaneously. Some are born with it so life is about having God tickle the base of your spine just to create a sensitivity, an awareness towards truth. That is all. It is a device that brings you to the essence of 'what is', which is what the definition of the word psychic relates to – leading to the essence. Previously this has only been seen within the spiritual context. The way that individuals are evolving within society now means that this can be seen in a greater light within the context of pure knowledge. Knowledge of your planet and solar systems, knowledge of your universes, knowledge of the galaxies and how they relate to each other within the universes. There is a wealth of knowledge about to be thrust upon the world. You have to be ready to receive it. You have to be prepared to listen. You have to be prepared to suspend your disbelief and entertain the most lateral of concepts. There is no need to invest in these concepts any belief, merely allow the mind to be empty enough to receive the concept and let that energy flow through the mind as it breathes, easy come, easy go. No effort. Your vessel often talks of doing nothing. He leads people in disciplined practice where they experience nothing. Try to understand the wisdom of this in relation to what we are saying. Experiencing nothing is illogical for you. But do understand that everything about your consciousness, your waking state of the mind, being able to experience absolutely nothing is the ultimate, because within this you are able to draw to yourselves what is required, that which is beyond your knowledge.

The Akashic Records are often defined as the library of everything through time. This is correct, as it relates to spiritual time and your emotional reality within this spiritual library means that you can have access to all emotional information, to all spiritual law, which can create greater awareness of the nature of Karma. If we say that one of the books in the library of the Akashic Records creates a vacuum that takes the individual into another dimension beyond emotional and spiritual experience, and that this particular book is closely guarded by certain individuals, and that only certain individuals can make this book available, so that, as more individuals come to experience the cosmic glory of the Kundalini, and more individuals are able to hold this book, then everybody can have access to this information collectively. This may not mean very much to you now, but it will. You are all in a very crude way being initiated into objective reality which allows the unconscious to float above the spiritual realm. Being able to vibrate above the spiritual realm allows you individually to have direct access to this cosmic blueprint without the need to be in the presence of a communication such as what we have here. You are being given a gift by being present at these meetings. Just allow that gift to assert itself. Allow those almost crazy impulses to expand within your mind. Allow those possibilities to grow. Trust, intuitively. Interpret what they represent for each of you as they will mean something different for each of you. You grow in your own light, in no-one else's light. Let that resonate within your minds for a moment. As that is the case, who do you listen to? As that is the case, who do you trust? As that is the case, who do you go to for understanding and teaching? As that is the case, can you really depend on any one ever again?

As we experience the shock waves that travel through

you with what we say, it gives you an idea, and only an idea, of what freedom really represents. Again, you can only see the minute scale in which this operates as you work from a very dense reality. But it also means that you have the facility to be able to move beyond that dense reality to get a sense of what is there.

You are entering a phase of your existence where there will be a two-phase experience of life. Those aware, and those who are not. Those who take life seriously, and those who do not. Those who depend on materialism for confirmation of their existence, and those who don't. The divide will become greater. This will create friction and pain, and it will bring about destruction. This is how it is. This is how it will be. You have to destroy to know what is real. You have to let go of what is comfortable and familiar to understand the essence of reality. You have to let go the old to create room for the new. So it is with your physical reality, and so it is ordained. Within the Kundalini condition, as there is a letting go of the spiritual, there is a greater embrace of the cosmic, and those individuals who embrace the cosmic will bring an appreciation of what it represents. Allow this to happen. Don't question it too much. Don't analyse the information too much. Allow yourself to experience the dynamic of this being, of this communication. Hold it in your hearts and let it be. Free yourselves from the impediment of knowledge. Honour your personal power as this is contained within your own light.

Are there any questions ?

*Is there a connection between Kundalini and electricity?*

In the way that you mean it, no. Both have a vital force,

however. There is no consciousness within electricity. It is purely a mechanical energy force. That is the difference.

*I would like to ask something from last week for clarification. When you have been talking about pulse and the origin of vibratory being you said it governs 40% of all that is. What would be the other 60%?*

It was divided up into three categories: pulse having 40%, light intensity having 40%, and the other 20% belongs to the divine force, even though pulse and light are divine at the level of divinity. It is very difficult to describe, to bring down to base emotional level. How can you divide God? But if we do divide God into three pieces: pulse, light and ultimate being, it is because the pulse and the light left, originally, its point of origin and will return eventually to the point of origin of which it was once a part. It is exactly the same, but there is a division, namely the pulse and the light have experience. The ultimate divinity does not. So even though there is no separation, there is a slight difference.

*I would like to ask one more question. Since beginning this course, it has been like I have not been well and yet on one level I know that I am well. I have a complete lack of energy. Is it connected to this course? Am I being forced into a state of just being?*

Words, as we have said, are often inappropriate. Yes, but we can offer no regret. Yes, and we express delight. Yes, and understand the magnetic resonance within cellular memory is being stimulated, which destroys dependency.

*Thank you.*

*I would like to ask is there any connection between certain beings being able to assimilate a high degree of cosmic understanding and certain individuals having a point of origin outside this particular physical universe?*

Yes, and the relationship is very direct indeed. To expand just a little more – for any impulse to experience something totally beyond its context, it has to have had experience of that context before. Remember, please, that you all individually and collectively, but particularly individually, have total freedom of movement. You can experience or move from one dimension to another. It is rare but it is possible, so depending on what context you relate this question to, we can only say yes. It has to be that way, otherwise there is no tolerance of that context whatsoever.

*Are we star-suited?*

If you mean are there consciousness forms or impulses living in the human context around the earth which come from other contexts, yes.

*I was specifically thinking of people within this room and also what would it mean to be star-suited – I don't quite understand it all.*

It is more to do with the multi-dimensional nature of your being. Your vessel talks about the counter personality in terms of your consciousness being operative now as we speak in different places within the universe, as well as here on earth, so that your ability to absorb information, multi-dimensionally, is more tangible. A very particular experience in a different place within your universe is very necessary. Not for everyone in this room, but for some people within this room, and for some people within this room, this has already taken place, even though there may not be any conscious awareness of it. It relates to what we were saying earlier about the freedom to move. In many ways, the races on earth reflect this. What we wish to convey has no real emotional resonance. It is best for us to keep this simple, I am just saying yes.

As we draw this evening to a close, take away the exchange of energy. Allow yourself to understand more fully perhaps the complementary nature of your being as it wishes to show itself, as it wishes you to experience. Be fluid and gentle in your approach with yourselves. Be alert in your appreciative nature. Energetically you will always stand between two pillars of vibratory force that will always give you access to what we represent even though you will not have contact with what we actually are. Until the next time.

# TEN

# *Cosmic Relationships*

As your understanding of humanity and your own personal position within humanity grows and evolves, you will find that you lose interest in yourself or in yourselves and humanity. Although this statement may seem rather extraordinary, it is the best way that we can describe the evolution of human consciousness. If you lose interest in humanity, if you lose interest in self-interest, it then means that your interest is directed elsewhere. This is a very positive reaction to this interest and it means that your focus of attention will then be directed to what creates even greater awareness, greater stimulation and greater understanding. This will cause you to relate to the physical universe, to try to grasp in a tangible way, fundamentally, how energy exists and communicates itself within the physical framework of that universe, allowing you to focus your attention on a particular star, on certain planets, and to understand not only how they relate but how they connect. It will cause you to examine the elemental construction or composition of each of these planets and stars, to understand how they may complement each other.

As your complementary medicine itself moves and evolves, it will come to a point when it will start to value more the essences that radiate from these stars and planets. The metallic elements that are contained within these certain physical points within the universe allow you consciously to draw on these elemental forces for well-being, both physiological and psychological. You will understand more and more how these frequencies contain and protect. How they also reflect vibrations which can be fractious for the emotional consciousness from the earth plane. You will use them in a very practical way to energise – not necessarily physically nor mentally – but energise in terms of motivation. Energise in terms of being able 'to be' within different dimensions.

As you view your consciousness, as you view your reality, it tends to be very cut and dried within the emotional, psychological and spiritual hierarchies. If you are to understand fully that the limitations of your psychological, emotional being are so small, and that, as soon as you are able to allow yourselves to remove or detach consciousness from this state of being, you will be given such flexibility as you could never possibly have imagined. This flexibility is now available around your environment and waiting for you to tap into. The structures are already in place to allow you to draw from them whatever you need. All that is required is for you to connect and draw, in a very direct way, from this strata of energy, which surrounds your solar system, into your being, which will cause a shift within you that will allow objectivity to draw you to a point where you are less involved in the crude rudimentary way in which you operate. This belt of energy doesn't circumnavigate the sun but extends outward and circulates around the outer ellipse of the solar system. If you regard the sun as the heart of your reality, this belt of energy cannot communicate itself through the heart, so it is not drawn through your sentient being, your feeling being, it is energetically drawn in, more through your clairaudient being. Your ability to hear. Your ability to know. Around this area of your being, there is little emotional context intruding on what you can know or can hear.

This band of energy is, in many ways, similar to your Milky Way, except it is more concise. It is denser than your Milky Way, even though it cannot be seen. It creates a resonance, and this resonance has to be passed through by any incoming consciousnesses that enters your solar system. This belt – let us call it a vascular being to reflect the vascular nature in your own physical body, the nervous system and the blood that circulates impulses and nutrients – this vascular layer that surrounds the outer limits of your solar system means that any incoming aspect of consciousness, as it passes through it, has to draw on a sense of progression that is cosmic in origin, alerting it to the fact that there is a database within the physical universe that can be drawn on. So when that incoming aspect or consciousness enters the physical state, it already has had an experience of this cosmic vibration. This belt has been in place for approximately fifteen of your years. It has not been wholly active except for the last six. Those beings who have been born within the last six years, have therefore had contact or experience of this belt of energy, this vascular system. So those, within the last six years, and indeed those that are to come, already have within them, within their genetic memory, a sense of this cosmic reactivity. We say reactivity because there is an instability here. There is a provocative quality that will cause their emotional body to vibrate more quickly. It then creates a sensitivity and an alertness towards humanity and towards the whole of life, that is going to create a dramatic separation. This separation represents a break-up of the emotional being, a break-up within your dense, physical reality, both of which bring about physical change and psychological change. Depending on the way that you perceive this, it will be equally as destructive as constructive. Always remember the principle that, whatever is taken away, has to be replaced by something else.

We are Izaris. We, within the cosmic sense, create balance, and we, within the cosmic sense, maintain balance. As we do this, in a totally non-emotional way, we work directly with your binary star, Sirius. We cannot speak for Sirius, but as we observe Sirius, what we see is a sense of cohesiveness being maintained between your emotional body and your physical, in your terminology, between your physical state and your spiritual state, so that there is a fluidity here. That means there is continuation of information and experience without block, without impediment, continually alerting you to the crystal consciousness that you have within. We have talked before about the nature of the crystal, and of the genetic quality contained within water. We have also talked about the progressive nature of how your bodies become crystalline. In some ways, Sirius has already achieved this, but having achieved it, it is now moving into a process where it is moving beyond crystal representation, so as it moves beyond, it is helping you to move from the physical to the crystal stage. We ourselves, as we maintain balance, hold within our vibrational atmosphere, mathematical crystals; the mathematical formulation that creates crystal consciousness itself. So what we have is non-matter representation of crystal consciousness as it is contained within Sirius, and Sirius has contained within it crystal consciousness of what is already in your own dense matter as it evolves. Then you have an idea of how the full picture relates.

Sauris, the consciousness that facilitates this communication, is merely the vehicle that promotes understanding, so within Sauris, the correct word for this consciousness is convenor. Sauris is the ambassador between Izar and Sirius. Sauris can maintain itself within both realities. If you regard Sirius as being specialised, and Izar as being specialised, then Sauris has complete understanding of both without needing to be specific to either. In terms of loyalty, however, the attraction is towards Izar. It would not be inaccurate to say that Izar promotes cellular growth, but then we have to examine the notion of cellular growth because we don't mean this purely within the physical sense of the word. If we know how your physical cell needs to evolve, then the energetic contribution that we have to make to that cell growth is enormous. We can't facilitate this on our own, which is where Sauris comes in, because what we understand is then transmitted to Sirius and it is actually Sirius, with the help of Chiron, that actually institutes a process of awakening within the cell of exactly what it needs, vibrationally, not only to maintain itself in times of change, but also allowing you, the human, to maintain a physical structure without rushing the process of evolution.

The cell, more and more, is becoming aware of its crystalline nature. The contemporary disease that you know as AIDS is creating a vibrational state within your immune system, where tiny crystals are being formed which magnify the virus within the physical body. AIDS reflects preparation, or the pre-cursor, to having a body which has no infections, which is going to be subjected to no physical infection. We say this merely to illustrate a point, rather than to suggest that those individuals who encounter AIDS are victims, or subjects of some form of experiment.

Although there is some form of preordination towards all life, you have to understand that within the context of your life there is free choice. Within the spiritual state there is free choice, so that, yes, there is a sense of 'I will allow myself to endure the learning process associated with AIDS because I understand the effect which that will bring in later time', and as long as you hold the whole context of what this means, you will allow the understanding to move through you without interruption. So that, if we are looking to 150 years hence, approximately, those beings who reincarnate within your environment will have within them the ability to deflect from them, or to burn up within them, any virus infection that comes their way, because the crystalline nature of their immune system means that any virus will no longer be able to tolerate being in such an intense vibrational substance.

You may already be thinking that if you, as humanity, reach a point where there is no disease, then there is nothing for you to learn through disease. Then, yes, it is quite feasible that your world will be disease-free. That is something that you need to understand and comprehend and come to terms with. Your science teaches you rather simplistically that, for every action there is an equal and opposite reaction. In terms of well-being and disease, every reaction that disease creates, as a learning process, may not mean that you will experience that reaction within the context of the same life or the same experience. That can come later, in a different time, in a different place.

Those individuals who are experiencing AIDS do so with enormous spiritual conviction and courage, consciously not always being aware of what they do. They will, however, experience the glory and the joy of living without disease in future time, as that is the reward for the sacrifice that they have already made. The crystalline substances that will be contained within your lymph system will be like tiny magnifying glasses, and as light, or the sun, shines through those magnifying glasses, they will burn up and destroy any unwanted intrusion into that physical body.

Within the reality of Sirius there is no disease. They are shimmering light forms of composite crystalline structure. By structure, we don't mean density, yet there is a certain form here, although it has no validity to it. The composite nature of the Sirian being allows it literally to take out or remove certain crystalline structures or cells from its domain altogether, so that any time that the charge becomes low or deplete, it is possible to re-charge those cells or those crystals and to replace them within the composite body without any sense of interference or degeneration. We cannot, realistically, give you an accurate description of how that affects us, as we are a disparate composition of consciousnesses which only come together momentarily to communicate something specific. We, in our way, do encounter uncomplementary vibratory states with which, sometimes, we have to cooperate and which leaves us feeling dislocated, without direction, needing to take stock and to heal, although not in the way that you experience or mean. And the way that we heal ourselves is through absolute stillness. As we focus on our vibration, it brings us into greater relationship with ourselves. It is not that the vibration increases – it does intensify slightly – but it is more to do with the deflection that is brought into our reality that we need to reassert our relationship with ourselves. So disease for us means losing sense of what we are and what we are meant to be.

The next fifty years for humanity will be about creating a bridge between the heart and the creative being. Creative being relates to the visibility you have in the world. In some small way it also relates to your occupation. This bridge means that you will live more in the creative being state and less in the heart. This doesn't mean that you are less compassionate or less feeling – in many ways you have a greater access and a greater sensitivity – but, as empathy is being removed from your reality, it will mean that you will be able to sense and know more intuitively, more instinctively, what's needed, and being able to respond to that in a very direct way without having to prove anything.

If you look at your Animal Kingdom it would not be inaccurate to say that your need to herd or be part of the group is becoming less. It leaves you more self-reliant, it allows you to understand more your own resourcefulness. This will cause you to lean less on others. You will still require companionship and you will still value friendship, but over the next fifty years, the sense of what that gives you will be something quite different. Friendship will be more about understanding, that there is someone who understands in a similar way. That doesn't mean to say that you have to be with that individual physically. Often, just by virtue of being there and being able to be experienced, the understanding will be enough. Those of you who come to the earth in fifty years time, if you don't understand that life is not purposeful, will no longer be able to maintain existence on earth, and will seek ways to terminate it by the time you have finished the first quarter of your lives. Again, we do not say this to shock, we merely say it to give you some sort of tangible understanding that your emotional state is evolving at such a rapid rate that you will not be able to tolerate restriction or fundamental pessimism within your being.

There are already those living around you who are gaining information vibrationally about what the earth requires in order to live on it with a sense of balance. There are already amongst you those who are understanding or gaining understanding of what, physiologically, the body will require from living on the earth in future times.

When you move into the middle of your next century, the word speed, or rapidity, will become extremely important. Speed, not only in terms of travel, but in terms of information, recycling information, sending information, experiencing information, will be very, very rapid indeed. Emotionally, your ability to hold onto this will be much reduced, so your need to have information will become less. You will experience more quickly, you will hold that experience within your being, and you will be able to put that experience to practical use. So, within the context of the physical brain, there is change. There is less density. We talked about the importance of the vibratory nature of the fluid within the spine and within the skull. This relates very much to the increase in speed that you will have in the middle of your next century. The vibration contained within the fluid is going to cause the softening of the brain stem as it comes into the physical brain. Yes, we can talk about separation of cells but we have to relate this to the connective tissue within the body and how this connective tissue will be restructured. By that we mean the way that nerve fibre passes through or surrounds connective tissue; how the vibrations physically pass through the connective tissue, so that, as the connective tissue becomes less dense, there is a greater immediacy within the structured body to be able to respond to a support mechanism that will allow bone structure to deteriorate – don't take that word literally – to find within it, namely, the bone tissue itself, the ability to produce mucus membrane that will structurally hold itself together in a completely different manner. This will allow you to manipulate your spine in such a way that will allow you to choose to be in a repose or an active mode. It is very difficult for us to explain exactly what is involved, but what we have is connective tissue playing more the role of bone, and the role of bone taking on more the flexible nature of connective tissue. Again, do not take this too literally. It is merely a device to explain how, within the physical structure of the body, greater flexibility will be instituted.

There will be a line of force connecting northern Britain with Ireland, going through Brazil, through Peru and Chile to New Zealand and the Antarctic. This line of force will not hit the Arctic. This line of force will create a weight that will change the elliptical nature of the earth moving around the sun. There is already a mechanism in place along this line of force, which will allow the earth to gently fit into a matrix of energy which surrounds the earth that will allow this elliptical change to take place. There will be very strong energy emanations, particularly off the west coast of Scotland, western Ireland, the interior of Brazil, the point where Chile and Peru meet in the Andes, and within the north west of the North Island of New Zealand where strong emanations of energies will arise. These are focal points for stellar energy to inject their reality into the physical earth. These areas are not heavily populated so the emanation that comes into these regions will make sure that the population is kept low here. People will be drawn to these areas, but only for short periods of time. Those who decide to settle where these energies originate will not always be able to maintain their reality in these areas, as the intensity that originates here will be too strong.

You may also find that there are irrational breaks in the

ozone layer within these places, so the intensity of light, indeed the ultra violet light will increase. The counterpoint of this line of force, as it continues around the globe in the opposite direction, will product a counterbalance, which will produce an earthing quality. This quality will require the assistance of many people who live along this second line of force, and the people who will choose to live along this line are those who have difficulty with evolved awareness as well as those people who feel they have a strong commitment to the mundane reality of humanity. This, in a simplistic way, will help in the redistribution of the population around the globe. It will also help create new land, which, over a period of time, will produce new flora and fauna and, conversely, will also bring about degrees of destruction and elimination of land and flora and fauna.

Within the parameters of your existence, you are perfectly balanced towards moving towards a new life, a new reality, a new purpose, a new existence. We merely come to make you aware, in as practical a way as we possibly can, of what may be involved and why. We do not seek to alarm but to instruct. We try to be as specific as we can, in terms of how this may be created. But to do so from our perspective often requires overly simplistic explanations. Take the feeling that is given with what is said and interpret very freely the literal words. Communication is flawed, the vessel is flawed, and the mode of receiving this communication is also reduced. To take into consideration, then, the irregularity means that you have to stay with the feeling evoked in you as to what change is about. The most important thing to remember in all of this is that fundamentally you are becoming something else. You are at a pivotal point of experience, which allows you, very precisely, to see the dropping away of the old and the embracing of the new, where, within your reality, there will be a resurgence of accelerating learning. Predynastic Egypt was the last occurrence of this effect. Now you are about to witness it again in your time. This time, there is a sense of conclusion, a resolution. The conclusion will bring you to a whole new state of being. This is when the rush really begins.

With the old Egyptians it was all very much about creating learning within the emotional context, understanding that the emotional context had not really been physically explored before. What predates predynastic Egypt does not really relate to the emotional condition. The density involved there does not relate to the life that you have now. Consequently what is to come will take you very much away from dense being altogether. It will allow you to experience the freedom of love, the freedom of joy, the freedom purely to experience in an uninterrupted way and within which there will be great clarity and understanding. It is important that you are aware of this and it is important that you are aware that there are certain structures in place that can allow you to experience that now. Beyond that, try not to allow yourselves to be pedantic. Try not to allow yourselves to hold on to physical information too much. The rapidity at which you will assimilate this over the next fifty years will teach you that this will not be possible anyway. So allow yourself to be immediately instinctive and inspirational, knowing that whatever comes is right and proper for you. Beyond that, it is not within our capacity to advise, but merely to command a sense of excitement towards the coming millennia and what will be contained within those millennia in terms of resolve and completion. Before we finally deconstruct our reality and depart, are there any final questions?

*I have one question. There is talk about the earth swinging on its axis. Is this going to happen in our lifetime?*

No, but it is already happening in a very minute way. In the way that you phrased the question, the answer is no, but it is already being implemented, it is already happening.

*You say you are going to deconstruct after this and that you reconstruct when you have information to impart. To reconstruct, how do you get the information, how do you know when to reconstruct? Is it something to do with vibrations or pulses which cause you to reconstruct here?*

When we say there is a degree of preordination it means that there is already through all space-time an impulse that wants to experience both balance and imbalance to give a greater sense of what it is. What itself actually is. In terms of our reality, there is always an alertness to balance. We do not choose to come together in a particular way, but whatever response is required will dictate what composition we take as we come together as a cohesive whole. So even though you give yourselves freely and consciously to coming together in a collective way, ours is not the motivation to do this. It is already in place.

*I would just like you to explain a little more about this diamond which is now around the sun and our system, which is affecting people born in the last six years and from now on. I'm a bit confused as to what the difference is going to be for them.*

As we explained, it creates a more rapid vibration within their emotional being, which ultimately will create a greater flexibility in terms of how they relate to life. But it will also create the opposite of that as well. As you move forward through time, if you use the image of the parting of the roads, then you encapsulate the reaction that will come from this band of energy. It is there to separate. It is not there to create cohesion. It is there to separate outmoded values, outworn beliefs, to bring about a sense of clarity and free-thinking to those who are prepared to operate in that way. Those who won't or can't will leave. Their time is finished. In many ways it is quite cathartic because it will give those who can't respond to their own progressive nature a finality, that will allow their own inner consciousness to leave the physical environment altogether and to operate purely from the realm of spirit.

*I should like to ask: if we find ourselves in a position to be able to visit the places of high energy emanations on and surrounding the earth, is there anything we should bear in mind to make the best use of the opportunity?*

Make yourself available and trust what you experience, as you may not always be able to relate that to anything you already know. But understand that, as you do allow yourselves to be available, you will be taken. If you have the courage to invite that into your life, or those specific vibrations into your life, know that they will come. But also do know that you will respond to what they represent.

*I would like to ask about the AIDS virus. I was at a workshop dealing with HIV and AIDS and the workshop leader mentioned the vibrational state and what was actually mentioned was he felt that each virus has its own consciousness – which seems to relate to what you were saying – and also that the majority of patients that he saw really did have spiritual courage, the very words that you mention. Are you saying that it is very difficult for the doctors and scientists to actually come up with some kind of vaccine or something to eradicate this virus, because it will be done on an individualistic basis? It is another way for humanity to heighten its vibration. It does seem that people who have this disease and who touch on their spirituality deal with it so much better, and this awareness almost controls the virus. It seems to slow it down, and they reach a certain balance within themselves.*

You make and understand your own observations as you speak which very nearly leaves us nothing to say. Medicine, the science which looks at the nature of this disease, looks at it linearly. To look at it non-linearly would be to look at it from a spiritual perspective. Those individuals who are suffering from this disease, as they do that for themselves, although not consciously, get a sense of their own solution as to what this disease means. This may not result in a cure but as that brings a greater quality of life, it can, as you say, slow down the process of physical death. But what that does, is make that individual more acutely aware of their consciousness, not only their life but their eternal life. As that registers more and more within them, it means that their ability to facilitate that understanding in future time becomes markedly better. It is not inaccurate to view this disease, as it enters each individual's body, as having a consciousness of its own, for it is so unpredictable. Yes, it is not inaccurate to look at it in this way. However, there is a collectivity about the awareness that it is trying to provoke within the consciousness of the world that is also important, mainly to try and remove from the disease all sense of morality and judgement. Within the framework of the psychological emotional condition, everything about the progressive nature of the world and humanity is about humanity on an individual basis. The only way each individual is able to trust their own innate sense of what morality means for them, is for them to have a clear sense of their own unconditional nature. In many ways for those who wish to respond in that way, that is precisely what any disease that brings about physical demise does, no matter what it is. We choose AIDS as an example because of the crystalline way in which the immune system will be reconstructed in future time for those particular individuals. Science will find a way in which to contain and to regulate this disease. The cure will come, but it won't come in a way that is expected.

We wish to withdraw. To leave as we came – silently, and non-invasively. To picture how we withdraw, imagine a multi-coloured flower, but as you examine each flower, you find that what you have is not a flower but a vibrating ball of consciousness and that as we disintegrate, each ball of consciousness freely goes its own way, so that eventually there is no whole but only aspects of the whole. So we will not communicate in this way again and the attraction that brings us into this form in the first place is now redundant. The aspects will always be, but the context of how we present ourselves now will never be the same again. You will know us. You will have contact with us. You will have a sense of what we represent. It merely leaves us now to open our beings, to leave you with a sense of what we are, as we feel it. As we know it. As we understand it, and as you will too. To allow yourselves to have access, or rather greater access to your beings, that is all that is asked, and all that is required, as what you have within you is perfect, is adaptable and very real. Trust it, love it and own it. It belongs to you and no-one else. Until the next time, in another place. We wish you well.